South Africa

CHALLENGE AND HOPE

South Africa

CHALLENGE AND HOPE

Revised Edition

American Friends Service Committee

Lyle Tatum, Editor

𝕀𝕙 HILL AND WANG

A division of Farrar, Straus & Giroux

Library of Congress Cataloging-in-Publication Data
South Africa, challenge and hope.
Bibliography: p.
1. Apartheid—South Africa.   2. Government,
Resistance to—South Africa.   3. South Africa—
Foreign relations.   4. Anti-apartheid movements.
I. Tatum, Lyle.   II. American Friends Service Committee.
DT763.S6425   1987   305.8'00968   86-29618

The AFSC gratefully acknowledges permission to reprint from the fol-
lowing: Atheneum Publishers for excerpts from *Asking for Trouble*,
Copyright © 1980 by Donald Woods; *Beeld*, Johannesburg; *The Economist
Newspaper Limited*, London; *Foreign Affairs*, New York; Harper and Row,
Publishers, Inc., for an excerpt from "The World House" in *Where Do
We Go from Here: Chaos or Community?*, Copyright © 1967 by Martin
Luther King, Jr., and from *The Riddle of Violence*, Copyright © 1980 by
Kenneth David Kaunda; Hill and Wang, a division of Farrar, Straus and
Giroux, Inc., for "Somehow We Survive" from *A Simple Lust*, Copy-
right © 1963, 1968, 1970, 1971, 1973 by Dennis Brutus; New Directions
Publishing Corporation for "I Am Waiting" from *A Coney Island of the
Mind*, Copyright © 1958 by Lawrence Ferlinghetti; *The New York Times*
for quotes from articles by Joseph Lelyveld (8/11/81) and Steven Lohr
(6/15/86), Copyright © 1981, 1986; *The Observer*, London; the *Philadel-
phia Inquirer* for excerpts from "Pennwalt Corporation" (May 23, 1986),
"Britain Banned" (May 24, 1986), "Some Hopeful Signs in South Africa"
(March 10, 1986) by Raymond Price, "GM to Stop Sales to South African Police and Military" (May 24, 1986) by Associated Press, and "Rohm
& Hass to Sell Division in South Africa" (May 22, 1986) by Larry Fish;
Random House, Inc., for excerpts from *Out of Africa*, Copyright © 1937
by Isak Dinesen, from *Waiting: The Whites of South Africa*, Copyright ©
1985 by Vincent Crapanzano, and from *The Covenant*, Copyright © 1980
by James Michener; *South African Digest* for an excerpt from a transcript
of a conversation between State President P. W. Botha and Dr. Frederik
Van Zyl Slabbert, November 25, 1985, printed in Supplement to *South
African Digest*, February 28, 1986; TransAfrica Forum, Washington D.C.;
University of Witwatersrand, Johannesburg

Contents

Introduction

Freedom is the theme of this book, specifically the heroic struggle for freedom in South Africa. The first edition of *South Africa: Challenge and Hope* was about freedom, and so is the second. During the five years since the publication of the first edition, much has happened in South Africa. The main change has been in the expectations of blacks* and whites.

The frightening intransigence of the status quo in response to the demands for change has become clearer. In spite of this, the hope for the end of white domination is no longer expressed in doubts but in terms of when and how. There are few blacks in South Africa so pessimistic that they expect to live out their lives in bondage. Even of those whites most resistant to change, few are so optimistic that they expect the "laager" to protect their privileges forever.

The rising expectations have intensified the struggle. There

---

*In this context, "black" includes those called African, coloured, and Asian. The term "nonwhite," formerly applied to this group, is no longer acceptable to blacks, as it defines them by what they are not, as well as using white for the frame of reference. As an indication of the unity of the oppressed, these three groups all wish to be known collectively as blacks. There is confusion, however, as in South Africa "black" is often used to mean only those most of the world calls African. In this book, "black" will be used only as a collective term for Africans, coloured, and Asians.

are many persons in South Africa working peacefully for peaceful change. But in the newspapers of the world there are almost daily reports of more persons being killed as the violence of each protagonist fuels the violence of the others. As reported throughout this book, there are more than two sides to the struggle, with ethnic groups, individuals, organizations, liberation movements, and others vying for power. There is a great variety of political and economic objectives in the mix.

The South African scene is highly volatile. Protests, killings, strikes, and other traumatic experiences are reported from all over that troubled country. Suggested changes in the laws supporting apartheid frequently make the news, but the suggestion may be implemented, dropped, or reversed. It is difficult to be accurate about the present, let alone forecast the future.

Challenge and Hope grew out of nearly fifty years of relationships with South Africa since the first visit by a representative of the American Friends Service Committee. For nearly thirty years AFSC has had staff living in southern Africa and assigned to work in various countries, including Zimbabwe, Zambia, Malawi, Mozambique, and Tanzania. Obviously, during many of these years these countries were colonial territories racially dominated by whites. AFSC found ways to assist in the political transitions and followed up with community development projects in the independent states. In addition to current community development in the field and educational work in this country on southern African issues, AFSC has assigned a representative to the SADCC countries (Southern Africa Development Coordination Conference) to try to find ways to assist in the objectives of the nine majority-rule states of southern Africa in working together on mutual concerns.

The first edition of *Challenge and Hope* was produced by a working party appointed by the Board of Directors of the American Friends Service Committee. After two years of research and writing by the working party, the Board of the

AFSC approved *Challenge and Hope* in April 1982 as a statement of its views on South Africa. The members of the working party were Harry Amana, Mary B. Anderson, Vincent Harding, Lewis Hoskins, Ann Stever, Lyle Tatum, and C. H. Mike Yarrow. Serving as staff consultants were Jerry Herman, Maghan Keitz, John A. Sullivan, and Bill Sutherland. We thank them for their work on the first edition and for the assistance a number of them have given in the production of this second edition. Among this group, Lyle Tatum should be singled out for a special word of thanks. Out of his deep concern for southern Africa and his experience in the region, which goes back to 1960, Lyle offered to assume a major role in preparing a new edition. He has given generously of his time and energy in revising, updating, and adding fresh material, and we are deeply grateful for his contribution, without which this edition would not have been produced.

AFSC issued a book-length statement on South Africa in an attempt to do justice to all parties concerned, all those both inside and outside South Africa who wish to understand and influence events within that country. To get beyond the action/reaction format of television newscasts, current events were examined within their historical and geopolitical context, with the aim of providing a better understanding of today's difficulties in South Africa.

This revised edition is true to the philosophy and perspective of the original edition but provides new information and addresses the issue of South Africa in its current setting. Statistics are brought up to date, there are revisions throughout, and Chapters 4, 7, and 10 are new. Chapter 1 presents the many facets of the system of apartheid, attempting to convey a sense of its pervasiveness and of what it means to live under that harsh system. The historical development of the current South African system is traced in Chapter 2. Chapter 3 tells the often untold story of black South African resistance to the growing power of the state over many years in the past. Chapter 4 brings the story of resistance up to date, reports on the South African government's response to that resistance, and includes information on other relevant current events. Chapters 5 and 6 discuss the interrelationships, political and economic, of South Africa with the rest of the world and with international organizations. The potential of these relationships for supporting positive change in South Africa is explored in Chapter 6. Special attention is given to the movement for divestment in Chapter 7. In Chapter 8 the struggle with the relevance of nonviolence to change in South Africa is discussed. Uncharted ways to discover new depths of commitment to peaceful social change and the creation of just societies are sought. There is no peace without justice. Chapter 9 proposes actions for moving toward a free South Africa, some focused on U.S. government initiatives, some for the U.S. public, and some for South Africa's government and people. The final chapter looks beyond the current struggle to the beginning period of a "one person, one vote" government.

The American Friends Service Committee believes that the problems of South Africa, like the problems of the United States, are at base spiritual, having to do with the sense of relationship to the divine, to the world around us all, to fellow beings, and to central beliefs. What people do politically is or ought to be an extension of the morality they profess. The spiritual ills of South Africa and of the United States are mirrored in the political realities of those countries. The moral responses to those realities will necessarily include actions of a political nature.

Stephen G. Gary
Chairperson
American Friends Service Committee

South Africa

CHALLENGE AND HOPE

1

Apartheid

South Africa is unique in building distinction
according to race into the foundations of its
political arrangements. Under the direction
of skillful politicians and a ruthless security
system, the fruit of this system has been
cruelty and deprivation as profound as any
known in this century.
—*Political Change in South Africa:*
Britain's Responsibility,
British Council of Churches[1]

Apartheid is South Africa's economic, political, and social
system which is based on race. It is buttressed by a complex
legal structure, security system, and theology that consolidate South Africa's wealth, power, and privilege in the hands
of a white minority. Its social impact makes apartheid one
of the most pervasive and oppressive systems the world has
known because it disfigures humans spiritually as well as
physically, the oppressors as well as the oppressed. In a land
of vastness, beauty, and bounty, apartheid is a tragedy that
twists, maims, and destroys the lives of its citizens, both
black and white.

The disparity created by apartheid is stark in such basic
things as land, education, and health. Fewer than 5 million
whites own 87 percent of the land and more than 24 million
Africans are assigned to 13 percent of the land.[2] This 13

percent is incapable of sustaining even subsistence agriculture under present economic and political circumstances.

The ratio of per capita allocation of government funds for education of white and African students, respectively, was 9:1 for the 1983–84 school year.[3]

The discrepancy in health care shows up in many ways. For example, in the 1984–85 budget $350,000 was allocated for treatment of alcoholism for Africans living in white areas (about 13 million persons). For whites (fewer than 5 million) the allocation was over $5 million.[4]

The apartheid system enmeshes all South Africans in a complex, interlocking web of restrictions which control and limit all aspects of life. For most Africans it means poverty, malnutrition, threat of imprisonment, violence, crime, poor housing, and separated families. It means the risk of freedom and life for those who challenge, oppose, or try to change the system.

The pillars of apartheid include the official identification of all citizens by race; the restriction of the franchise to white, coloureds, and Asians for a parliament with built-in control for whites; restriction by race of areas for ownership and occupation of land and housing; segregated, unequal education and health systems; and restricted personal and social interaction among groups. Apartheid is enforced by a range of wide-reaching security laws, applied by police and military forces at the discretion of government leaders, the police, and minor officials. While individual laws making up the structure of apartheid may change, the system must be seen as a whole.

Racial Identification

In South Africa racial identification determines all facets of a person's life. It determines minor aspects such as the bus stop at which to stand while waiting for the segregated bus; it determines major aspects such as the quality of education a person receives and the location of home and work; it determines economic, social, and political rights.

The Population Registration Act of 1950 ensures that every person is assigned to a racial category—white, coloured, or African. Since Asians (mostly Indians) were considered undesirable foreigners, they were not categorized separately. In practice, however, there are separate administrative departments for Asians in relation to education, residential and commercial areas, and wages. Africans are further divided by ethnic group. Coloured people are those of mixed racial background, many tracing their heritage to the seventeenth century when the Dutch settled in Cape Province.

The South African government has established boards which determine classification and may change it. The process of reclassification is usually traumatic and humiliating,

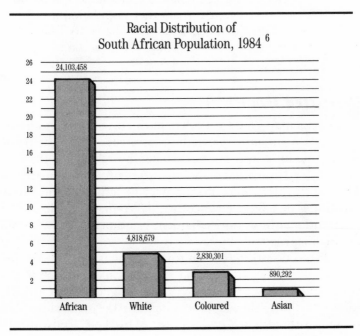

Racial Distribution of
South African Population, 1984 [6]

since the basis for change includes family history and physical characteristics, such as the width of the nose or the type of hair. It has resulted in the separation of husband and wife, of parents and children, or sisters and brothers, since people of different races must live, learn, work, and travel separately. Between July 1, 1982, and June 30, 1983, 690 persons had their race classification changed by South African officials.[5] Racial identification continues in 1986.

"Chinese persons will in future have the same status as Whites in respect of the Group Areas Act," the Minister of Community Development, Mr. Pen Kotze, said in Parliament recently. . . .

"After enactment of the Bill, all Chinese persons will have precisely the same rights and status as Whites except where a Chinese person has married someone from another population group.

"Then that Chinese will have to live in the marriage partner's group area," he said.[7]

Restricted Franchise

Africans may vote for leaders in the townships and homelands and for members of ethnic councils. Given the nature of these political institutions designed by whites for the black majority, Africans have shown little enthusiasm for them. These institutions have little power or influence and do not constitute an effective voice in government. There is little constitutional limit on Parliament's authority, and it retains the final legislative power.

In 25 elections for African town councils in 1983, the percentage of voter participation varied from 5.9 to 36.6. The average was 21 percent, as compared with 30 percent in 1978.[8] Many of those elected to councils in the townships have subsequently resigned under pressure by their "constituents" who see them as collaborators with the government.

Coloureds and Asians have been even less enthusiastic about their newly won right to vote for members of their own race to serve in racially segregated divisions of Parliament. Of potential voters in the Asian community, 16.2 percent voted in the first election in 1984. Of the coloureds, 18.1 percent of the potential number voted. In the Cape, where the most coloureds live, only 11.1 percent of the coloureds voted.

The limitation of the franchise to whites, now partially changed, developed during this century. Until 1936 some Africans in Cape Province could vote for members of Parliament, although only for whites. It wasn't until 1956 that coloureds were removed from the common electoral roll in Cape Province.

There are no elections now (November 1986) at any political level where a person can vote for anyone outside his or her own racial classification.

Land

Historically and systematically, apartheid began long before its proclamation in 1948. Its roots are embedded in the issue of land. British settlers and Afrikaners, the whites of Dutch and Huguenot background, realized that land was the key to any scheme of development in South Africa. This realization prompted the expropriation of African land, early by conquest, later by law. The 1913 Natives Land Act denied the right of Africans to buy white land and vice versa. This made a de facto division along the lines of land usage at that time. The division is still maintained by law, with 87 percent of the land reserved for whites and 13 percent for Africans. The Native Trust and Land Act of 1936 attempted to restrict Africans to the reserves, although millions of Africans continued to live in urban areas and on white farms as agricultural workers either in compliance with influx control provisions or illegally.

These laws preceded the 1950 Group Areas Act, which

proclaimed strict residential segregation and became a cornerstone in apartheid's legal and economic structure. The Group Areas Act declared that South Africa was composed of African, coloured, Asian, and white areas, and that each group had exclusive ownership and occupation rights within those areas. The 87:13 ratio was maintained; occupation was defined from the most temporary kind (such as "occupying" a movie theater) to living in an area. The Group Areas Act is the foundation for the strict segregation of South African society. No black may own property in a white area; no black may occupy such land without special permission. The African areas were further divided according to ethnic differences among the African population.

Indians and coloureds were primarily affected by the Group Areas Act, as Africans had been restricted previously. Indians and coloured were allocated restricted areas within the white areas for their homes, shops, schools, and hospitals (all segregated, of course). This entailed a massive uprooting and resettling process, which is not yet completed. Some whites were moved, but the comparative numbers speak eloquently of those who bore the heavier burdens. By the end of 1983, 2,331 white families, 39,892 Indian families, and 82,859 coloured families were moved under the Group Areas Act as reported by the South African government.[9] A well-known resettlement case is that of District Six of Cape Town. The district had been occupied by coloureds since 1834. In 1966 it was proclaimed a white area, and coloured families were ordered to move. At that time the estimated population of District Six was 60,000 coloured, 800 whites.

Such numbers pale to insignificance when compared to those for African resettlement. The number of Africans who have been forcibly moved is a hotly contested statistic in South Africa. The government admits to the removal of 2 million people.[10] The Surplus People Project, a private group which spent three years studying removals, reports more than 3.5 million Africans moved.[11] Another 1.5 million were scheduled for relocation but were reprieved by a change in government policy. However, removals continue under a variety of justifictions. On October 17, 1986, the South African government announced the closing of Oukasie, an African township which is fifty-five years old. Ten thousand persons will be forced to move to another township. Most of these removals are to the homelands discussed below. Between 1960 and 1980 the proportion of the African population living in the homelands rose from 39.5 percent to 54 percent.[12] The urban dweller who is resettled to a homeland may never have seen it before and have no ties there. No consultation or choice is involved when a resettlement order is given. The South African government insists that residential segregation is needed for racial peace. It has, in fact, brought distress and tension in both urban and rural areas.

Law and practice often differ in South Africa for practical or humanitarian reasons or just bureaucratic inefficiency. There are, for example, countless thousands of Africans living illegally in African urban areas, and coloured and Indians rent property in white areas. But at any moment the law may be enforced inhumanely and efficiently.

The South African government is in the process of making the ten homelands "independent." In 1976 the Transkei became the first homeland to be granted "independence" by the South African government. It has been followed by Bophuthatswana in 1977, Venda in 1979, and Ciskei in 1981. KwaNdebele is scheduled for "independence" in December 1986. "Independence" is a controversial issue in Kwa-Ndebele, and in August 1986 the KwaNdebele legislative assembly voted to reject "independence." Development projects which were intended to celebrate "independence" upon completion are continuing, and the South African government has not responded (as of November 1986) to the KwaNdebele legislative assembly vote. If the vote is not reversed, "independence" will probably be delayed until KwaNdebele makes a new request for it.

No nation in the world but South Africa has yet recognized any of these homelands as independent states. Most of the homelands do not even consist of single geographic units (see map on page 32). Bophuthatswana is made up of seven unconnected areas. There are about fifty separate areas of KwaZulu. There is little prospect that the homelands can be made economically viable. They receive 85 percent of their regular budget from the South African Parliament on an annual basis. A 1980 study by the South African Council of Churches refers to a development plan for Venda, prepared for the government in 1979. The minimum cost was estimated to be R94.7 million (94.7 million Rand) per annum from 1980 to 2000. (The Rand on October 24, 1986, was worth $0.44.) South Africa would have to advance 80 to 90 percent of that.

After five years of "independence" George Matanzima, Prime Minister of the Transkei, said: "South Africa is not really interested in the development of Transkei. South Africa intended it to be a labor reservoir."[13] The South African Council of Churches reports:

> According to the Quail Report released on Feb. 20, 1980, Ciskei had 19% more people in the 0–14 and 65-plus age groups than South Africa at large; an unemployment rate of 39%; subsistence farming output of about R40 per head per year; and a resident gross national product of R180 per head per year, most of it derived from wage earnings in South Africa—where white per capita income averages R2,500 per year. "The most desired form of government (ninety per cent of all Xhosas polled) was a unitary state for the whole of South Africa on a one man, one vote basis. This was the most favoured solution right across the board on the part of urban and rural Ciskeians, old and young, male and female, poor and richer, traditional and detribalized."

The evolution of the bantustan to "independence" is a basic implementation of apartheid. The South African government now has only nominal responsibility for the "independent" homeland, while in the past it was directly responsible both politically and economically for the bantustan.

The change is a reflection of the South African government's attempt to put a new face on apartheid. The ultimate goal of "separate development," as it is now called by the government, is the creation of African "independent" states. Africans would then have political rights and citizenship in their own "states," and would be left without even a claim to citizenship or political rights in South Africa itself. This situation is true already for those whom the government decrees are "citizens" of the "independent" homelands, whether they have ties there or live in a city hundreds of miles away. Citizenship is removed from South African residents by an act of the white Parliament or by administrative fiat.

Extensive protests about the loss of South African citizenship, and the fact that passports issued by the homelands are not recognized for international travel, have caused some rethinking of the citizenship issue by the South African government. Some form of dual citizenship will probably evolve.

The homelands are reservoirs for the maintenance of cheap, controllable black labor. The population of the homelands is primarily the old, the sick, the very young, women, and men waiting to find work. Wage earners leave for work in the mines, the urban industrial areas, or on white farms, sometimes hundreds of miles from their families. The wage levels are rarely enough to support the workers' families adequately, even with supplementary subsistence agriculture in the homelands.

The problem of survival is compounded by the high population density of the homelands. Inadequate wages and the attempt at what is less than subsistence agriculture in the homeland produce a life with health problems, nutritional deficiencies, and high infant mortality. Inflation affecting basic costs such as food hits homeland Africans especially hard because of their limited resources.

Africa and the international community remain seized with the continuing problem of the racist system of apartheid. The deleterious effects of the inhuman system are borne by all oppressed people in South Africa and Namibia, especially women and children. But equally many women of South Africa and Namibia have risen with determination, courage and heroism to resist and fight apartheid, alongside their men, in a bitter struggle which has intensified within the period of the United Nations Decade for Women (1976 to 1985). However, it is impossible to consider women's problems in isolation, their solutions must be sought within the destruction of the political, economic and ideological framework of the entire apartheid edifice.

—*Women and Apartheid in South Africa and Namibia,* United Nations[14]

Women and Apartheid

In every society women hold certain positions and perform certain functions different from those of men. Many of their roles are often related to the support and nurturing of children and to maintaining households. When poverty is extreme, as it is in both the urban townships and the rural homelands of South Africa, the burden on women is especially heavy. A series of regulations, laws, customs, and cultural expectations confine many women to the barren soil of the homelands, where they must attempt literally to scratch some life from the land. Because of influx control, the limitations of rights, and a severe shortage of urban housing for them, only one-fourth of African women in South Africa are engaged in paid employment; most others are confined to the homelands. These depend on the meager wages which can be earned in the cities and sent back to them by their husbands to feed, clothe, and house the children who are in their charge.

The number of African women who are wage earners, however, is growing. When they enter the paid labor force in South Africa, they experience additional hardships. They, as well as the men, are separated from their children, even the newborns, as a condition for living and working in restricted white areas. They are paid less than men in virtually every occupation. In 1984 it was estimated that 50 percent of the female African work force was concentrated in domestic service, 18.6 percent in agriculture, 12.8 percent in factory production, and 11 percent professional (largely teachers and nurses). Most jobs held by African women are low-paid and few are subject to regulation regarding minimum wages, work hours, or even minimal benefits such as sick leave or paid holidays. Since legislation enacted in 1981, all women who are covered by a minimum wage have been protected against sex discrimination in wage levels, but few are covered.

Recognizing the particular susceptibility of domestic workers, the South African Institute of Race Relations* has a project to organize domestic workers to standardize wages and to improve working conditions. This project works with white women employers as well as with black domestic workers.

In addition to the usual handicap of inferior education under apartheid, few African women have had an opportunity for higher education. In primary and secondary education the number of boys and girls in school is approximately equal. After that level, there is a stark difference. According to *Women and Apartheid in South Africa and Namibia,* a report by the United Nations Economic Commission for Africa, there is only one African woman civil engineer. Also according to that report, in 1984 there were no African women trained as lawyers, judges, or pharmacists. Although women carry

---

*SAIRR is a private, voluntary organization, based in Johannesburg, which does excellent work on race relations and the collection of factual information and publishes an annual survey on race relations.

much of the burden of manual labor in agriculture, there were none with a professional degree in agriculture. In contrast, women members of the African National Congress (ANC), outside of South Africa, have qualified in many professions.

In the liberation struggle, the challenge for women is twofold. While they seek freedom for their people, they also seek within that freedom equality with men. Women's organizations in community affairs have traditionally been strong in South Africa. In the 1940s women campaigned for food rations and attempted to organize food cooperatives when food prices were rising rapidly. In the early 1950s African women organized "cultural clubs" as alternative schools during school boycotts. Black women have also been active against resettlement and squatter removals. In 1978 at Crossroads and in 1980 at Phoenix township, near Durban, women led resistance against removal in ways that received international attention. Women actively resisted the extension of pass laws to them.

Both the Pan Africanist Congress and the African National Congress have strong policies on ending not only sex discrimination in apartheid but the sex discrimination of South African culture, black and white. ANC observed 1984 as the Year of the Women of South Africa.

The United Democratic Front is the largest and most representative anti-apartheid organization within South Africa. Mrs. Albertina Sisulu, President of the Federation of South African Women, was elected Joint National President of UDF while in prison for her work against apartheid.

Control of Black Labor and Movement

The Stallard Commission in 1922 (twenty-six years before the National Party came to power) stated: "It should be a recognized principle of government that Natives—men, women and children—should be permitted within municipal areas insofar and for so long as their presence is demanded by the wants of the white population."

In other words, Africans were seen as "labor units" to be kept in the rural areas unless needed by whites in the cities. The policy of anti-urbanization of Africans was enforced, in part, by the pass laws.* Although they went through various legislative changes, pass laws in South Africa go all the way back to the days of slavery in Cape Province. A primary part of the modern pass was the employment record, showing that the "labor unit" had a right to be in the city where employed.

The pass laws have been replaced by a requirement that identity cards be carried by all racial groups. Identity cards carry the owner's photograph, but no statement of racial classification. Just how the new identity cards will be used by the police is uncertain. In spite of serious doubts about the effects of the elimination of the pass laws, the ending of arrest and imprisonment of hundreds of thousands of persons for pass law violations is welcome.

A severely limited supply of housing and highly restrictive regulations on eligibility for housing constitute another method used to keep Africans out of the cities. Until mid-1986, no African could stay legally in a "prescribed area" (white area) for more than 72 hours unless he or she:

a) was born in the area
b) had worked for the same employer continuously for ten years or different employers for fifteen, and had lived in the area with no breaks
c) was the wife, unmarried daughter, or minor son of a qualified resident, as in a) or b)
d) had permission from a labor bureau

These qualifications were set out in the Black Urban Areas Consolidation Act of 1945 (three years before the National

---

*For a report on pass laws, see *South Africa: Imprisonment under the Pass Laws* (New York: Amnesty International USA, 1986).

Party came to power), and are commonly named for the section of the act which spelled out the qualifications, Section 10 rights.

Few women qualified for Section 10 rights on their own. Thus women who had lived in an urban township for their entire lives as dependent daughters and wives were subject to removal if their husbands died, deserted them, or divorced them. Late in their lives, with no means of sustaining life, many women found themselves removed to the homeland of their former husbands, where they had never been and where they had no family connections at all.

Men were often given employment without authorization for family housing. In some cases families have remained together illegally. A highly publicized case was Crossroads, a creation of women and children. Crossroads is a squatter community outside Cape Town where women and children illegally joined the men who were working in the area. National and international pressure and demonstrations prevented the government from removing the squatters and destroying their shanties at that time. But the case is exceptional. In August 1981, three thousand people, mostly women and children, were arrested at another location in Cape Town and, under a law which applied to non-South Africans, were sent back to Transkei, where many faced the possibility of malnutrition or even starvation. Employment for many Africans causes the destruction of normal family life.

What the abolition of restrictions on the movement of Africans will mean in practice remains unclear. The State President has stated that there must be "orderly urbanization." Part of what he means by this is that racially segregated housing areas will be maintained, and Africans will not be allowed to move into cities unless they have approved housing. There is already a severe housing shortage for Africans in the cities, with estimates of "illegal" residents in Soweto, not to mention the many other townships, possibly as high as a million persons. It is not uncommon to have twenty persons living in a four-room house. A strict enforcement of zoning laws, which might require one family to a house, would greatly reduce the population of urban Africans while a legal façade of free movements of people is maintained.

Apartheid has resulted in gross disparities in income for labor, with the gap in earnings continuing to grow. The continued spread in actual earnings is shown in the chart below.

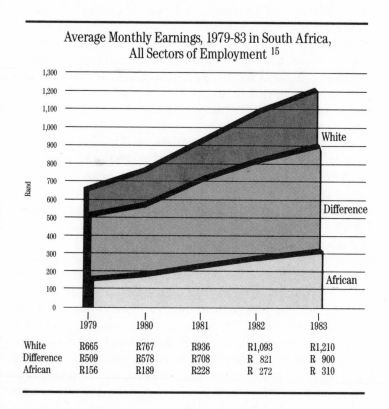

Average Monthly Earnings, 1979-83 in South Africa, All Sectors of Employment [15]

	1979	1980	1981	1982	1983
White	R665	R767	R936	R1,093	R1,210
Difference	R509	R578	R708	R 821	R 900
African	R156	R189	R228	R 272	R 310

Education

Another key element in apartheid is the education system. Until 1953 education for Africans was offered by the central government, provincial governments, the churches, and communities. This provided a considerable variety of approaches and quality. Many African leaders in the rest of southern Africa were educated in some of the institutions in South Africa.

In 1953 the Bantu Education Act was passed, centralizing responsibility for education. Hendrik Verwoerd, then Minister of Native Affairs and later Prime Minister, introduced the bill saying: "When I have control of native education I will reform it so that the natives will be taught from childhood to realize that equality with Europeans is not for them." And later: "What is the use of teaching a Bantu child mathematics when it cannot use it in practice? . . . Education must train and teach people in accordance with their opportunities in life."

The resulting quality of education for Africans has been a major source of frustration. Until the 1980s education was both free and compulsory for whites, but neither for Africans. African schools have been overcrowded and understaffed, and the curriculum has reflected Verwoerd's principles. In 1984, the teacher/pupil ratio for whites was 1:19 and for Africans 1:41. In one homeland the ratio was 1:68.[16] Due largely to the 1976 Soweto uprising, which initially focused on the deficiencies of the education system, the Bantu Education Act was replaced in 1979 by the Education and Training Act, No. 90. The Act provides for the gradual introduction of compulsory education, free tuition, and free schoolbooks for Africans. While the amount spent on African education has been rising steadily, there has not been the massive increase in the national education budget necessary for implementation of the Act. The priorities were made clear by Minister of National Education Punt Janson in 1980. Defending the superiority of white education, he said: "We want to give white education the very best, and then we want to give the other people the best possible in the shortest possible time."

The Education and Training Act also provides that children will be educated in their ethnic language for the first four years. While this might appear educationally sound, it does not take into account the situation in South Africa. To teach in an ethnic vernacular, of which there are eight to ten in South Africa, when many children attend school for only four years, is to promote separation among Africans and to prevent many from learning a language that is more broadly used.

The Act does address the issue of whether subjects will be taught later in English or Afrikaans, a question with intense emotional impact. Parents will be able to have a say in that choice.

Nevertheless, these reforms do not touch the basic issue of the quality of education for Africans. African families are deeply concerned about the devastating and stunting effect of the education system. Many sacrifice time and money to find ways around the system. They turn to voluntary organizations to help fill the gap and meet needs through night schools, short courses, and technical training. Private schools meet the needs of a few. In 1986, there were 5,142 black students in 169 private schools with about 50,000 white students.

Major school boycotts and protests by coloured and African pupils from 1980 on until an uneasy truce in 1986 indicate that change in education remains a primary issue. Both groups want a unified national education system. Posters in one of the 1980 demonstrations read: "Down with Tribal Education, Divide and Rule" and "South African Education Stultifies, Denies the Right of All to Grow Fully, Think Freely, and Develop Our Potential." At the 1980 annual conference of Headmasters and Headmistresses of Private Schools of South Africa, the group agreed to send a telegram to Mr. Janson urging "the establishment, after consultation between all affected parties, of a unified, nonracial system of education which protects the individual rights of all South Africans." Pressure for change is being exerted by children, parents, and educators. The De Lange Commis-

sion report of the Human Sciences Research Council, sub-
mitted in late 1981, recommends further reforms. Yet there
seems to be little change in the basic system, which prompted
a U.S. Congressional Study Tour (July 3–11, 1980) to report: "The South African government has used education as
a political instrument to keep black South Africans in a
semipermanent state of ignorance and economic deprivation."

Restricted Social Interaction

The social lives of all South Africans are restricted by the
apartheid system. The Prohibition of Mixed Marriages Act
of 1949 and the Immorality Act of 1950 and 1957, which
sought to control the most intimate of relationships, have
been repealed, but neither those laws nor their repeal had
much effect on the lives of most people. While there has
been some relaxation in the segregation of sports due to international boycotts, laws such as the Group Areas Act in-
hibit integrated sports. The relaxation takes place through
the use of permits or by nonenforcement of laws rather than
by a change in the law, which would indicate a yielding on
principle.

We can never remind ourselves too frequently just
how blasphemous a creed apartheid really is. It
seeks to do nothing less than obliterate the image
of God in a large part of humanity. Firstly, it denies black people the right *to be*. It forces them to
conform to an image which the Master Race has
created of them. . . . This philosophy of black
inferiority is enshrined in South Africa's laws and
customs and prevents the black people from being
themselves—themselves not as whites see them but
as God has made them. . . .

Secondly, apartheid denies its victims the right
to belong. Through its policy of racial segregation,

it imposes unnatural divisions on society, choosing a quite irrelevant standard, that of skin pigmentation, to fix the boundaries of community. . . . It is morally indefensible, economically mad and politically explosive. . . .

Thirdly, apartheid denies its victims the right *to have*. The Charter of the United Nations Organization lays down certain fundamental human rights which all persons possess for no other reason than the fact they are human. . . . Every man, woman and child has a right to a place at the feast of life and the main policy drive of any enlightened nation must be to reduce those inequalities which rob human beings of their chances through no fault of their own.

—Kenneth Kaunda[17]

Hotels and restaurants may serve blacks as well as whites, but few do so, other than the most expensive. Whites need permits to enter African areas. Few whites ever witness life in the townships. In fact, few South African blacks and whites meet except in a master-servant or employer-employee relationship. Social interactions are severely restrained by law and custom. The rich potential of a variety of human relationships in South Africa remains untapped.

Enforcement and Security Laws

The South African government has enacted a series of laws to enforce the apartheid system and to prevent change. Most basic are the Suppression of Communism Act of 1950, the Terrorism Act of 1967, and the Internal Security Act of 1976. These laws support the state in almost any action to neutralize or destroy opposition. "Communism" and "terrorism" are defined broadly by the South African government. In the Internal Security Act, the definition of Communism includes any doctrine which "aims at bringing about any political, industrial, social or economic change within the Republic by the promotion of disturbance or disorder, by unlawful acts or omissions," or which "aims at the encouragement of hostility between the European and non-European races of the Republic" where the consequences are calculated to further the kind of changes defined above. Peaceful but effective resistance campaigns are thus defined as "Communist." The Terrorism Act is even broader, and includes as terrorist acts "to cause substantial financial loss to any person or to the State" or "to embarrass the administration or the affairs of State."

Detention without charge is a major tool used by the South African government to suppress dissent. From 1963 to 1967 detention became legal for 90 days, then 180 days, and finally for an indefinite period. At this time, a person merely suspected of terrorism, as defined above, may be held without charge or trial for an indefinite period of time, at the sole discretion of a police officer of the rank of lieutenant colonel or above. The courts are expressly prohibited from intervening. In 1976 a law was passed authorizing the Minister of Justice to detain any person he suspects of being a danger to the state security or public order, even without dependence on the broad Terrorism Act.

In all cases, detention may include solitary confinement and torture. Winnie Mandela was held in solitary confinement in the late 1970s for seventeen months. She was never charged with a crime. In January 1982 she was served with her fifth five-year banning order. Now (mid-1986) released from the banning order, she speaks out fearlessly at the risk of being arrested again.

Banning is a method used to silence critics of South African government policies and the apartheid system. The Internal Security Act authorizes banning, a totally arbitrary procedure, with no recourse or appeal. No reasons need be given. Most banning orders restrict a person for five years and can be renewed. They prohibit the person from speaking publicly, being quoted, and entering educational institutions, publishing houses, or courts. The orders commonly restrict the number of people a banned person may see at one time, usually to one. A banned person is usually not allowed to leave a magisterial district. Normal employment or social life is generally impossible. Banning orders are served primarily against blacks, but whites are also banned. The extensive bannings of October 19, 1977, included that of Donald Woods, a white newspaper editor, and Beyers Naudé, a white Dutch Reformed minister and founder of the Christian Institute, which challenged apartheid.

The threat of detention and banning, both arbitrary and unchallengeable procedures, resulting in anything from social isolation to death, is an effective means of intimidating those who would criticize or change the apartheid system. There have been a number of deaths among political prisoners in detention. Dr. Neil Aggett, a white union leader who was reported to have hanged himself on February 5, 1982, was the first white to die in detention.

Biko was a nonentity until he died. Only after his death did the media, the left and the enemies of South Africa, following the pattern of the Nazis with Horst Wessel and the communists with Patrice Lumumba, raise him from obscurity and make him into a martyr.
—Martin Spring, *The Star* (Johannesburg), February 11, 1984.[18]

Among blacks, the death of Black Consciousness* leader Steve Biko is one of the better known. He was detained on August 18, 1977, in good health. Twenty-six days later he

---

*The Black Consciousness Movement believes that black groups and black leaders bear the responsibility for the liberation of South Africa and the advancement of black people.

was dead. These grim facts are not disputed by the South African government:

1. Biko was held naked in solitary confinement from the 19th of August to the 6th of September.
2. He was taken to the interrogation room on the 6th of September. That night he was handcuffed and shackled by leg irons, locked to the walls, and left to sleep that way.
3. He was not removed from the irons for two days, by which time he was mentally confused; his hands, feet, and ankles were swollen and cut; his clothes and blankets were soaked in urine.
4. He was taken naked in the back of a Land-Rover 750 miles to a prison hospital. He was given a mat and died on the stone floor of his cell.

The chief magistrate of Pretoria absolved the security police of any responsibility, and the South African government has never admitted any irregularity in Biko's treatment. A medical panel of private physicians, eight years after the death, found two government doctors guilty of falsifying medical records and giving Biko inadequate care. One doctor was reprimanded. The other was barred from medical practice for three months, but the penalty was suspended. Biko was the twenty-fourth person to die between March 19, 1976, and September 12, 1977, while being held in detention without charge in South Africa.

Fifty-two persons died in detention in South Africa between 1963 and 1978, according to an annual report of the U.S. State Department on human rights abuses.[19]

During the violent year of 1985 in South Africa and up to the temporary ending of the state of emergency on March 7, 1986, about 1,500 persons were killed and 8,000 detained. At least 11 died in detention.[20] Deaths in detention continued after the end of the state of emergency, with 5 deaths in April 1986.[21]

Those in opposition to the regime are often frightened with threats, wearied, harassed, and even killed. The system seeks to break them by the security apparatus and a fearsome petty bureaucracy.

The security system is enforced by the police (nationalized), by the special Department of National Security, and by the military. There are, however, other means of controlling opposition to apartheid. There is extensive control of the press. While criticism of the government does appear in the press, there are actually quite extensive limitations on its freedoms. "The appearance of a healthy press and liberty of expression is false," said Anthony Matthews, a Professor of Law at the University of Natal in Durban. Pressure is maintained on the national press association to police their members regarding stories with "negative racial overtones." The Defence Act of 1957 and the Official Secrets Act prevent publication of any unauthorized information about the South African military. Because of these laws news of the South African Army's invasion of Angola in 1975 was not published in South Africa until long after the rest of the world knew about it. The Police Act of 1958, amended in 1979, makes it illegal to publish articles criticizing police behavior. The Prisons Act of 1959 forbids criticism of prisons. Newspapers can be closed and lose their R20,000 registration deposit, as has happened to several African papers, the *World* in 1977 and the *Post* and *Sunday Post* in January 1981. Donald Woods, exiled South African journalist, explained in his autobiography: "The Government had at its disposal more than twenty statutes governing what could be published in newspapers, and several of these laws empowered them to close down any newspaper arbitrarily, without court proceedings, and to jail or ban any editor without explanation."[22] The banning of TV coverage in the townships during the state of emergency has been widely reported.

The Steyn Commission of Inquiry into the media made recommendations in early 1982 for further restrictions and control. These included the licensing of journalists and the setting up of a government-controlled council to monitor and discipline journalists. These recommendations were not enacted into law, but the threat is clear. Self-censorship by the press is the result.

The government can also outlaw organizations under the Unlawful Organizations Act of 1960. Eighteen organizations were so banned in October 1977, losing their property to the state. Under the Riotous Assemblies Act of 1956, amended in 1974, the government can forbid meetings and gatherings, either private or public, consisting of two or more people.

The South African government uses a wide variety of tools to prevent changes in the apartheid system. They range from intimidation to control of information and to overt violence. The laws permit wide use of unchallengeable discretionary power, leaving the opponent of apartheid under constant threat, and keeping government officials increasingly out of touch with the level of anger and bitterness of the people, as well as with the strength of demand for change.

In the face of the pervasive system of apartheid, its denial of human values, its ruthless enforcement system, the human spirit remains indomitable.

Somehow we survive
and tenderness, frustrated, does not wither.

Investigating searchlights rake
our naked unprotected contours;

over our heads the monolithic decalogue
of fascist prohibition glowers
and teeters for a catastrophic fall;

boots club the peeling door.

But somehow we survive
severance, deprivation, loss.

Patrols uncoil along the asphalt dark
hissing their menace to our lives,

most cruel, all our land is scarred with terror,
rendered unlovely and unloveable;
sundered are we and all our passionate surrender

but somehow tenderness survives.

—Dennis Brutus[23]

Whites and Apartheid

The South African government has been controlled by the National Party since 1948. This party is dominated by Afrikaners who formally and deliberately brought apartheid into being. But its roots go back to the Act of the Union in 1910 and earlier, and will be more fully discussed in the next chapter. Here we note that the foundation of apartheid can be found in the culture and religion of the Afrikaners, as well as in its pragmatic acceptance by the English-speaking part of South Africa's white population.

The Afrikaans word *apartheid* (pronounced a-par-tate) means "apartness." The alleged purpose of the policy is to maintain cultural identity for the Afrikaners and others. In this theory, separation is the natural way of life because it allows groups to develop in their own way, with their own customs and languages. Hence the term "separate development" is now often used officially instead of "apartheid." It is clear, however, that the promotion and protection of Afrikaner culture is based on white control of land and resources, of politics and economics. Whites must dictate where and how others develop. Afrikaners seem to believe that their cultural survival is synonymous with their domination and control of South Africa. The religion of the Afrikaners is Dutch Reformed, a Calvinistic form of Protestantism, which is discussed more fully in the next chapter. That religion contributes to a sense that Afrikaners are a "chosen people," with both mandate and responsibility to dominate and control South Africa.

Cultural preservation and religion are mixed in the Broederbond, a society of "brothers" formed in 1918 to promote
the interests of the Afrikaners. In 1928 it became a secret
society. Various exposés of the society indicate that its
membership is exclusively white, male, Calvinist, and Afrikaner. Since the National Party has been in power, there
has been a remarkable overlap between the Broederbond and
the highest officials in government, in the Dutch Reformed
Church, in education, in the media, and in the civil service
and transportation system. The "brothers" have served as
the ideological architects of the modern South African state
and as the chief promoters and defenders of apartheid. Debate on policy is reported to take place in both the Cabinet
and the Broederbond Executive Committee. The fact that
most of the Cabinet members are "brothers" makes it difficult to delineate their roles clearly. Thus, the government
is deeply influenced by a secret society, committed first and
foremost to the Afrikaner people and their interests. While
there have been disagreements within the Broederbond, a
high priority is placed on a united front in defense of the
state. The secret society has stifled any move toward inclusion of the vast majority of South Africa's population in the
decision making.

Apartheid as a coherent theory was conceived by Afrikaners. Yet some of its key policies or directions were developed while the English-speaking whites were in control of
South Africa, up to 1948. Apartheid is still supported by
many of the English-speaking population. They have shown
little initiative or leadership in the political arena to challenge the National Party. Until recently, they held a monopoly on the economic power in South Africa, a power
based on their control of rich natural resources and on cheap
labor. Many thus actively participate in the exploitation of
South Africa's black population and resources. Others in-
sulate themselves from the horrors of apartheid and support
the paternalistic view of Afrikaners that whites know best,
will care for blacks, and therefore deserve to stay in control.

All who benefit from apartheid become its accomplices, despite verbal protests to the contrary.

It is also true that most white liberals emerge from the English-speaking population. But many Africans question how far such liberals will go in supporting fundamental change. In 1980, for example, white liberal students supported the school and university boycotts. But when threatened with expulsion and denial of their degrees, they returned to classes. Not so the Africans and coloureds, who faced similar penalties. While many English-speaking South Africans oppose apartheid, few seem ready to give up their privilege as part of the necessary transformation of their society. The contribution of whites who resist and criticize apartheid should not be ignored. It must be acknowledged, however, that the system has been supported by the vast majority of English-speaking whites as well as by Afrikaners. There are encouraging signs that public opinion is changing. Whites are moving away from support for apartheid in the sense of social and economic racial discrimination. There is, however, little white support for "one person, one vote" for all of the citizens of South Africa.

Apartheid, as a deliberate public policy, has given race a class definition. Whites are South Africa's upper class, and blacks are the lower class. Apartheid has assigned to the white portion of South Africa's population, on the basis of its physical characteristics, control of all the political mechanisms of the state, the dispensation of the gains of the majority's labor, and the ultimate power to chart and direct the cultural and social interaction of the entire nation. It is a system of rigidities, resisting the organic growth and constructive changes found in most societies.

The rigidities of apartheid seem to be weakening. One who should be an authority, South African State President Botha, has declared apartheid to be dead. However, black leaders are still asking to see the corpse. None of the "reforms" hailed by South African politicians in power has touched the essence of apartheid. Opportunities for employment in an integrated workplace with black foremen, access to restaurants, even abolition of pass laws do not dent apartheid.

As Rev. Brian Brown, a courageous South African pastor, put it cogently in a speech at York on April 16, 1986: "The name of the game is not concessions. The name of the game is power."

Only when blacks are given, or have taken, political power in proportion to their numbers will apartheid be dead.

Those opposed to apartheid tend to see it in terms of its tragic impact on blacks, for it is blacks who bear most of the oppression. For whites also, however, apartheid has serious negative effects. There are whites, both Afrikaners and English-speaking, whose opposition to apartheid has caused them to be banned, imprisoned, harassed by their fellow citizens, and killed. Some of these have felt it necessary to go into exile.

Such impact on whites is easy to see, but apartheid has negative effects even on those who support it. There are dehumanizing consequences of the oppression of people and a psychological price for racial arrogance and separation. There is a deprivation from lack of friendship on the basis of equality with persons of rich cultural diversity.

White South Africans of all shades of political opinion carry feelings of guilt, fear, and defensiveness which become evident in the most casual conversations with visitors when apartheid is mentioned. Apartheid is a burden for *all* South Africans. And the resulting violence, explicit and acute or implicit and chronic, damages all.

2

Roots of Crisis and Hope

Apartheid in South Africa today can best be understood through a brief review of the historic forces that have molded the present society. The recent story is one of conflicts among people with different ideologies, group interests, and national designs, all rooted in the past.

The history of South Africa properly begins with the emergence of humanity on the continent. But the concern here is with the recent era that gave rise to the problems—political, economic, and human. Whether one regards this story as depicting the conquest of a subcontinent and its economic development by European settlers or the struggle for survival by Africans as dignified, self-defining people against the encroachments of foreign invaders, the theme of conflict between European and indigenous people has persisted from the mid-seventeenth century to the present. How did it develop? When did the rivalry for territory become explicit racial exploitation? This will be summarized with a focus which is Europocentric, reflecting the way in which South African history is generally recorded. The Chronology following Chapter 10 outlines the developments.

The arrival of the Europeans to stay began at the Dutch provisioning station on the Cape of Good Hope in 1652. The area was then populated by nomadic peoples, the

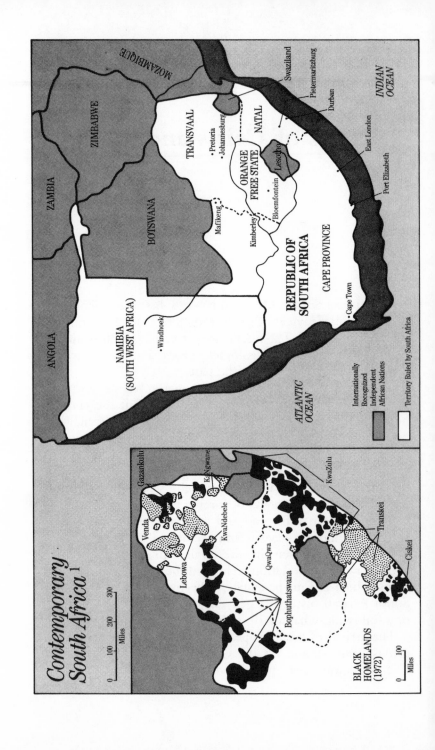

Contemporary South Africa[1]

Internationally Recognized Independent African Nations

Territory Ruled by South Africa

ATLANTIC OCEAN

INDIAN OCEAN

ANGOLA

ZAMBIA

ZIMBABWE

MOZAMBIQUE

NAMIBIA (SOUTH WEST AFRICA)

BOTSWANA

Windhoek

REPUBLIC OF SOUTH AFRICA

CAPE PROVINCE

TRANSVAAL

ORANGE FREE STATE

NATAL

Swaziland

Lesotho

Pretoria

Johannesburg

Mafikeng

Kimberley

Bloemfontein

Pietermaritzburg

Durban

East London

Port Elizabeth

Cape Town

0   100   200   300
Miles

BLACK HOMELANDS (1972)

Gazankulu

Venda

Lebowa

KwaNdebele

KaNgwane

QwaQwa

KwaZulu

Bophuthatswana

Transkei

Ciskei

0   100
Miles

Khoikhoi (often called Hottentots) and the San (often called Bushmen). Their eastern neighbors were the migratory Bantu-speaking peoples, notably the Xhosa, Zulu, Tswana, Sotho, and many smaller ethnic groups. Despite official statements about "an empty subcontinent," the evidence is clear that representatives of these black groups were already occupying large portions of the greater Cape area. The Dutch soon expanded beyond the original station for the Dutch East India Company and gradually developed a settlement area for Europeans wishing to start fresh in another temperate part of the world. Over time, the company controlled, curbed, or displaced the indigenous people to provide for arriving European settlers. There was resistance to this presence almost immediately (see Chapter 3).

The early colonists were much influenced by their religious origins. Most of the Dutch were committed Calvinists, adhering to the theology of the Reformed Church. Their numbers were later augmented by the arrival of Huguenots who were fleeing their French homeland after the revocation of the Edict of Nantes in 1685, which for a century had permitted religious pluralism in that otherwise Catholic land. The Huguenots merged into the Dutch population and, as Calvinists, became members of the Dutch Reformed Church. Both groups left Europe prior to the French Revolution and in their isolation rarely felt the influence of liberalizing ideas that originated there.

As the numbers of Europeans increased, the competition for land and cattle with the much more populous indigenous Africans grew more intense. By the eighteenth century, the San, to escape annihilation, had retreated into the Kalahari Desert. The cattle-herding Khoikhoi were more willing to accommodate, but no successful *modus vivendi* in the economic competition could be achieved. They were pushed into the interior and decimated by ruthlessness and disease. During a century of close interaction at the southern tip of the continent, the mixing of the races produced the "Cape coloured" population. But to the east the larger number of Africans were much more inclined to resist European incursions into what they felt was their territory. Thus "frontier wars" marred the late eighteenth century, much as "Indian wars" long occupied North Americans. The frontier line moved slowly eastward, and later northward as white military might drove African farmers and herders back.

Typical European use of grazing areas (staking out of portions for individual use) brought them into frequent conflict with the nomadic Africans who used the communally owned grasslands for their herds in the traditional manner. The clashes between the two groups resulted in the Dutch (now Afrikaners*) accumulating more cattle and subjugating Khoikhoi as servants or slaves. Afrikaner nationalists look back to the late eighteenth and early nineteenth centuries as the beginning of a clearly defined emergence of European communities tied to the African land. While maintaining a strong identification with their European heritage, they relinquished their ties to a specific homeland and established a pattern of intense independence.

A common identification as Christians helped to unify the Europeans against the numerous African ethnic groups of the area. Indigenous people felt the increasing pressures of European encroachment, both physical and psychological. Missionaries brought a religion new to them that raised fundamental challenges to their traditions and tended to divide them. Many indigenous people accepted Christianity, some adapting it to their religious customs, while others held to their traditional beliefs. Other Christian denominations were represented among later European immigrants. The importation of Asian laborers in the nineteenth century brought Hindus and Muslims from India, adding to the rich religious mosaic and to divisions among racial groups.

---

*At that time the Dutch were known as Boers (farmers). For convenience we will generally use the present-day term, "Afrikaner."

Advent of the British

At the turn of the nineteenth century, international politics intervened in South Africa. As part of the Napoleonic Wars, the British first occupied Cape Colony in 1795 and became permanent residents in 1806. The territory was ceded to the British by Holland in 1814. In 1820 the British began to send in colonists, many of whom were ex-soldiers, who established settlements along the coast to the east of Cape Town. British colonial political control made the Dutch settlers restive, due partly to the emergence of nineteenth-century British liberalism. Impositions included making English the official language in 1828 and the abolition of slavery throughout the British Empire in the 1830s. These two changes weighed heavily with the Dutch in South Africa as infringements on their economic and cultural activities. The Dutch had already begun a rather extensive exploitation of the indigenous population and had imported slaves from the Far East and East Africa. They also feared they would lose their language and cultural identity. In great resentment, many Dutch settlers moved eastward and northward in an attempt to escape British hegemony. This great trek of 1836 became known as the "Voortrekker Movement."

The trek and the conflicts that it generated, coupled with Afrikaner psychological and religious needs, molded a people, a "Volk." The links that were forged created an Afrikaner legend which supported their belief in their right to conquer the lands and people that lay before them.

The Afrikaners wanted to achieve a utopian society as a "chosen people" dedicated to God. The Bible, especially the Old Testament, became their guide and defense. But their desire for isolation was soon thwarted. The discovery of diamonds in Kimberley in 1867, followed by that of gold in the Transvaal in 1884, attracted large numbers of chiefly English-speaking fortune hunters. The indigenous Africans, already exploited by the Afrikaners, now suffered under the encroachment of the British. To the Afrikaners, this influx of aliens seemed impious and coarse, threatening their way of life. But they could not stop the invasions. The "mineral revolution" that followed transformed South Africa from an economically marginal area into an important participant in the world capitalist economy and an increasingly industrialized nation. The country was led in this direction by mining magnates, such as Cecil Rhodes, who became involved in the politics of southern Africa, hoping to extend British imperial control northward.

The rivalry between the British and the Afrikaners culminated at the end of the nineteenth century in the second Anglo-Boer War (called "Boer Wars" by the British, "Wars of Freedom" by the Afrikaners). In conventional warfare, armaments, and manpower, the British always had the upper hand, but the Boer commandos, organized into effective guerrilla units, fought fervently for their homes and freedom. The British responded with a scorched-earth policy, which brought great suffering and many deaths to the civilian population. Large numbers were put in internment camps. After fierce and prolonged fighting, the British prevailed. In 1902 they offered the Afrikaners a reconciling peace (which has been characterized by some persons as an attempt by the British to salve their consciences). Yet the bitterness of the conflict produced an enmity that has never completely disappeared. Some of the generosity of the peace terms came at the expense of the Africans, for the terms reestablished absolute Afrikaner control over the local African population in the Orange Free State and the Transvaal. African leaders protesting this control were ignored. Also ignored were liberals and anti-imperialists in Britain, many of whom had opposed the war from its beginning, who generally supported the reconciling peace terms but were ineffectual in securing rights for Africans.

The Union

The Union of South Africa (now the Republic of South Africa) was created in 1910, with four provinces—two predominantly British (Cape Province and Natal) and two Afrikaner (Orange Free State and Transvaal). The Union was more than a loose federation of relatively autonomous provinces, since the central government could control all areas. It was in fact operated by coalitions led by Afrikaner generals. Though the Union remained a British territory, English-speaking citizens tended to turn to business, mining, and commerce, leaving Union politics by default to Afrikaner intellectual and religious leaders, such as General Jan Smuts, who worked through the United Party.

From the end of the Anglo-Boer War until 1948, when the Afrikaners finally gained control of the government, the most intensely nationalistic sector of the Afrikaner population set as its goal the recovery of their traditional Volk unity and power through cultural and political efforts. Loosely bound together by cultural affinity and their sense of grievance, they formed a growing political strength. Their population expanded more rapidly than that of the English, adding to their majority status. They were able to cooperate in political organization and maneuvering. The successful National Party, in power since 1948, was the result. Their leaders sought to free South Africa from the "yoke" of British imperial control; the first step of achieving dominion status in 1926 was confirmed in the Statute of Westminster in 1931. The Declaration of the Republic in 1961 finally ended British political responsibility. The referendum on the Republic was in fact passed by a tiny majority of white South Africans. The Afrikaners' long-standing desire for complete independence was heightened by their discontent at being drawn into a "British imperialist war" in 1939, and they were increasingly uncomfortable in a British Commonwealth of Nations which now included black nations. A change from Union to Republic required a reconsideration of membership in the Commonwealth. Prime Minister H. F. Verwoerd soon discovered in 1961 that black members of the Commonwealth would reject any reapplication, so none was made, thus ending all formal national ties with Britain.

By midcentury, Afrikaner leaders were beginning to diversify their economic base. While many remained attached to the land, an increasing number entered commerce and industry. Financial institutions appeared, catering to their constituency. The professions—law, teaching, investment counseling, and others—attracted Afrikaner young people. This brought them into contact with their English-speaking counterparts and the wider world of business and international finance. Some even began to see that the restrictions of the apartheid system were handicaps to their capitalistic ventures. For example, businesses were prevented from hiring black workers except for menial roles. This added to their labor costs when they had to pay artificially high wages to white workers. Few, however, abandoned their commitment to the National Party, where ideology overruled economics (as in the United States South in the early days).

The party was bolstered by Afrikaner economic strength, based on farmers, miners, and industrialized blue-collar workers. The better-off members of the party tended to join the affluent urban dwellers who enjoyed the fruits of a thriving economy. This prosperity was based on abundant resources, the inflated value of gold, a patronizing government that usually protected white (Afrikaner) workers, diversification, and a seemingly limitless supply of cheap black labor. Their religious and cultural tradition interpreted their advantages as rewards for faithfulness to ordained rules and as their rightful destiny. Blinded to or unaware of the suffering of the majority, aware of their own earlier hardships and disadvantages, and increasingly alarmed by the danger of losing their way of life, Afrikaners voted for the continuance of the system. In fact, the vast majority of whites in South Africa today, Afrikaner and English-speaking alike, still vote for "continuance of the system." There is, however, a sharp difference of opinion between those who want the old system without change and those who think some degree of liberalization might make it possible to continue white domination.

The Dutch Reformed Church

The church has long been a prime factor in preserving and building Afrikaner culture. This culture comprises the new Afrikaans language, the Reformed religion, and other aspects of "tribal memory," reinforced by the record of recent persecution and earlier the experience of concentration camps established by the warring British forces, into which women and children were herded, 26,000 of whom died during the Anglo-Boer War of 1899–1902. Preachers from the pulpits and theologians imbued with bitterness produced a negative doctrine toward the world outside but a close and often warm and generous relationship with their own. They built up the strength of the faith, the theology of separation, and belief in the purity of their race and their ethnic group within the white community.

By six in the afternoon, fires would be blazing. It was so beautiful. We all knew one or two families, and they would bring us lovely sausages, homemade boereworse. My sister and I would look forward to it. On Saturday morning there would be an enormous bazaar, or so it seemed to us then. And in the afternoon there would be an auction for the benefit of the church. Even in 1933, during the terrible drought, there was a sheep that fetched over five hundred pounds and a cake that fetched over a hundred pounds! Those farmers used to bid on a sheep and once they got it, they would

auction it off again. This year we made almost
five hundred pounds—and from poor people who
gave more than a tithe.

> —An Afrikaner woman's memories,
> quoted in Vincent Crapanzano,
> *Waiting: The Whites of South Africa*[2]

The church's traditional isolation from European thought
was scarcely modified. Since contacts with the motherland
were severed, Afrikaners, until World War II, tended to be
"platteland farmers."* What the devout Afrikaners saw of
the urban, predominantly English-speaking communities
repelled them. Their clergy insisted that they retain traditional rural values and their distinct culture, emphasizing
strong family ties and their profound religious heritage. Not
involved in urban commerce, they turned more to politics.
Their political organizations, most of which had a strong
religious bent, operated on the British parliamentary model.
This trend culminated in 1948 in the capture of the Union
government by a militant wing of the National Party. Their
first Prime Minister, Dr. D. F. Malan, was a dominee, or
minister, of the Dutch Reformed Church (DRC). Many of
the Cabinet members and most of the Prime Ministers were
trained at the Afrikaans-language University of Stellen-
bosch. Their political platforms reflect strong religious and
theological views.

The Dutch Reformed Church must not be seen as an "established church" like the Anglican Church of England, yet
the alliance of government and church strengthened the
commitment and outreach of both. "Daughter" missionary
Dutch Reformed churches grew among Africans, coloureds,
and Indians in the twentieth century, as did activities of outreach and service, not only in the Union but beyond to

---

*Literally, "lowland or flatland farmers," a South African term referring to the
expanses of relatively level land farmed by many Afrikaners.

neighboring areas. But contrary to the experience of other churches, the Dutch Reformed Church was never in favor of an integration of congregations, theological schools, or synods. The black churches were intended to be completely separate, though their leadership was provided from the European or white clergy.

Eventually theological training schools were set up for the blacks. All instruction was in Afrikaans and led by Dutch Reformed white professors. Church leaders did not foresee that the black theologians would soon rise to prominence as they became local preachers and missionaries in the rural areas and also in some of the growing urban locations. Nor did they anticipate the startling new development that the Nederduitsche Gereformerde Sendingkerk (coloured), the Reformed Church of Africa (Indian), and the N. G. Kerk in Africa (African) would all opt for independence and become essentially nonracial.

Today liberal white Dutch Reformed Church members in some cases prefer to worship with racially integrated groups. These congregations are now speaking out courageously on social issues, to the discomfiture of their former mentors.

The white Dutch Reformed churches have resisted "reform" and have retained their insulation, having refused since 1960 to participate in ecumenical bodies such as the World Council of Churches and the South African Council of Churches. Earlier attempts to cooperate were short-lived, for the DRC encountered criticism for its support of apartheid from its more liberal Protestant colleagues and for its ecumenicity from more conservative congregations. South African Calvinists even mistrust church leaders in Holland for their liberalism. They dismiss the growing protests of church people all over the world as the expression of "liberalists" insensitive to their social circumstance.

The coloured congregations were an anomaly because their leadership and rank-and-file membership spoke Afrikaans and were culturally so close that they were often regarded as "brown Afrikaners." They too, however, were expected to retain separate congregations, churches, synods, and schools. Gradually white Dutch Reformed Church ministers were replaced by coloured preachers.

Conservative white Dutch Reformed Church leaders participate in the Broederbond (see Chapter 1), thus reinforcing the "political theology" of apartheid, mixing cultural preservation with religion. In 1945, Professor Cronje of the University of Pretoria wrote: "The racial policy which we as Afrikaners should promote must be directed to the preservation of racial and cultural variety. This is because it is according to the Will of God, and also because with the knowledge at our disposal, it can be justified on practical grounds." The rhetoric may have been modified of late, but not the practice. The reference to the Will of God is part of the Calvinist heritage of the Dutch Reformed Church. Afrikaners rely heavily on the Old Testament as well as on a Calvinist sense of mission or predestination. Some have identified themselves with the Children of Israel as the "chosen people" and with God's elect. They regard the survival and prosperity of their small groups as evidence of God's favor, and their electoral victories from 1948 to the present as mandates of God. As a "chosen people" they see themselves appointed to lead all of South Africa.

There have always been exceptions to these generalizations. Outstanding Afrikaners have left the church, often joining the newly independent formerly "daughter" churches, to oppose apartheid policies generally endorsed by their denomination. Although there are three major groups within the white Dutch Reformed Church, exhibiting distinct theological and cultural differences, their tendency to support the government has been consistent until recently when concern about blatant racism began to develop.

Other Religious Communities

Since the middle of the twentieth century a number of the Christian denominations inside South Africa have become more outspoken in their criticism of official policy, especially at the upper leadership level. Some have moved toward mixed congregations, church services, and schools, though most are still far from integrated. Closer collaboration among churches with different ethnic traditions follows the experience of considerable ecumenical cooperation in the creation of post-secondary-school institutions like Fort Hare University, Adams College, and the Federal Theological Seminary, all of which were taken over or otherwise threatened by the government when they appeared to be centers of radical student activity. The Seminary had to move, but it is surviving.

The Roman Catholic Church takes a strong position against apartheid. The Catholics have given up government subsidies and continue to operate integrated schools at their own expense.

Since midcentury the South African Council of Churches (SACC) has exercised growing influence, not only on ecumenical activities but in coordinated efforts against apartheid. Most denominations, aside from the white DRC groups, either are members or, like the Roman Catholic Church, cooperate with its programs. In the 1970s and 1980s, leadership in the SACC has moved toward black churchmen. Bursaries (scholarships) aid promising scholars from all ethnic groups to continue their studies. Conferences and workshops are organized on religion and social issues. Publications provide stimulus to discussions in congregations and church schools. Current issues concerning detentions, migratory labor, family life, and nonviolent social change are addressed. The recognition of the rights of conscience has been fostered. Representations are made to authorities on religious and humanitarian issues.

The Christian Institute, now banned, is an example of an ecumenical, interracial church movement that inspired many Christians, especially younger ones, to vigorous, cooperative action opposing racial discrimination. It published studies and inspirational messages for practical use. It stimulated political awareness throughout the country and brought blacks and whites together in common endeavors.

Groups other than Christians have significant representation in South Africa. Only 6 percent of the Indians are Christian; most of the others are Hindu. South Africans may also be Muslim, Jew, or Confucian. Non-Christians, plus those who claim no religious affiliation, make up 25 percent of the population. The other 75 percent classify themselves as Christian.

Persons of other than the Christian faith, particularly Hindus, have been active politically as individuals, though the organized religions of which they are a part have not. Many Jews in South Africa have opposed apartheid, thereby exposing themselves to the latent anti-Semitism of some Afrikaner nationalists, who may have carried it over from sympathy with Nazis during World War II. Israel's votes against apartheid in the UN have brought criticism in South Africa. Growing economic and trade cooperation, however, as well as a shared sense of being surrounded by hostile states, have brought South Africa and Israel closer together.*

Namibia

Since World War I, South Africa has extended its power over neighboring Namibia (called South West Africa until recently). South West Africa was administered as a German colony from 1884 until 1915, when South African forces invaded. Germans had settled in the area, living along the coast and in the better-watered lands of the north-central plateau. Prior to World War I, African resistance led to a German order of extermination, in which 50,000 to 70,000 Herero and Nama were killed and their land and cattle confiscated. The remaining people had little choice but to work for whites.

---

*For further details on religion in South Africa, see Marjorie Hope and James Young, *South African Churches in a Revolutionary Situation* (Maryknoll, N.Y.: Orbis Books, 1981).

After the end of World War I, the League of Nations gave to South Africa the administrative authority over South West Africa as a mandated territory. Article 22 of the Covenant of the League of Nations states: "The well-being and development of such peoples form a sacred trust of civilization." South Africa reported annually to the League of Nations' Permanent Mandates Commission until the collapse of the League in 1939. During this time South Africa violently suppressed rebellions by various African groups—the Ovambo, who make up half of Namibia's black population, the Nama, and the Rehoboth people, called Basters. South Africa also imposed restrictive legislation on South West Africa, including regulations controlling the movement of "natives" and the creation of "reserves" where "natives" were to live. These reserves were mostly on poor agricultural land in the south or in the sand of the Kalahari Desert. From the beginning, the intent of South Africa seemed to be to absorb the territory.

After World War II the United Nations created a Trusteeship Council to take responsibility for the League's mandated territories. South Africa contested this action, and other former League members and the UN General Assembly sought an advisory opinion from the International Court of Justice. Both this ruling and another one twenty-one years later came down against South African control. In 1971 the International Court reached the following conclusions about Namibia: "that the continued presence of South Africa in Namibia being illegal, South Africa was under an obligation to withdraw its administration immediately and thus put an end to its occupation of the Territory; that UN members and nonmembers were under obligation to recognize the illegality of South Africa's presence in Namibia and to refrain from acts which might imply recognition of the legality of South Africa's presence and administration." South Africa ignored this ruling, as it had the previous one.

From 1946 to 1966 the UN set up a number of committees and initiatives to deal with South Africa's role in South

West Africa. In 1966 the General Assembly declared South Africa's mandate over South West Africa terminated and placed the territory under the direct responsibility of the UN. In the same year, the South West African People's Organization (SWAPO), organized in 1960 as a nationalist liberation movement, began its armed struggle for independence. In 1967 the General Assembly of the United Nations established the UN Council for South West Africa as the only legal authority to administer the Territory until it gained independence, and appointed a UN Commissioner for South West Africa. In 1968 the territory was officially renamed Namibia by the UN. Just as South Africa refused to accept the termination of the mandate, it has also ignored UN machinery to administer Namibia. Important recent developments on Namibia are reported in Chapter 6.

Thus, for most of this century, South Africa has controlled Namibia, in the face of increasing world disapproval. It has extended its apartheid rules and security legislation as well as its military power to Namibia, where the South African Defence Force operates.

While South Africa remains reluctant to grant independence, the people of Namibia seek world support. Before being sentenced to Robben Island, the Namibian leader Hermann Toivo ja Toivo said from the dock in 1966: "We feel that the world as a whole has a special responsibility toward us. This is because the land of our fathers was handed over to South Africa by a world body. It is a divided world, but it is a matter of hope for us that it at least agrees about one thing—that we are entitled to freedom and justice."

3

Amandla Ngawethu!

> We shall not win our freedom except at the cost of
> great suffering, and we must be prepared to accept it.
> —Albert Luthuli, *Let My People Go*[1]

Today in South Africa, in a barren hall or perhaps in an open field, the successor to the African herdsman of 1652 raises a clenched fist and shouts the Zulu word *Amandla* (power)! His listeners raise clenched fists and shout the Zulu word *Ngawethu* (is ours)! The recognition by Africans that power ultimately lies in their hands marks the beginning of the end of more than 325 years of white domination.

This chapter briefly examines the historical resistance by blacks to white domination. The next chapter reports on resistance in the more recent past and the present.

1652–1900

The Dutch East India Company's need to obtain a regular supply of fresh meat, fruit, and vegetables for the trading post and for transient ships was met by enlarging the frontier community with settlers willing to farm. There were cattle raids by settlers and by Africans. Seven of the first twenty-five years of the history of whites at the Cape were marked by what have come to be known as the Khoikhoi wars.

As the settlement extended east and north, displacing the

Khoikhoi and the San, both Dutch and British whites came into conflict with more militant Africans, such as the Xhosa and the Zulu. The last twenty years of the eighteenth century were marked by frontier wars. Africans had neither guns nor horses. The superior technology of the whites gave them the major military victories, and they took the land by firepower.

In the first half of the nineteenth century, the last great warrior chieftains of the area which is now South Africa, Mzilikazi of the Ndebele and Dingane (or Dingaan) of the Zulu, who ruled large territories and subjected many tribes, were ultimately helpless against the Boers' superior weapons. Mzilikazi and Dingane captured quantities of livestock and killed trekkers on the front edge of the invasion. Dingane killed a detachment of some seventy Boers led by Pieter Retief, but it was Dingane's troops who were slaughtered at the Ncome River, renamed Blood River (Bloedrivier in Afrikaans), December 6, 1838.

The Battle of Blood River in 1838 became a great legend in Afrikaner history. It was there that Afrikaners, faced with superior numbers of African warriors, promised God that if they won they would make a covenant with Him to hold this land for their posterity. Their superior firepower prevailed, and they interpreted their victory as God's will.

That battle marked the last military action large enough to be called warfare between the Afrikaners and the Africans until the current guerrilla war with SWAPO on the Namibia–Angola border. The last annexation of African territory was that of Pondoland in 1894.

The period 1652–1900 was a time when southern Africa was torn with many violent conflicts. Africans were striving for territorial control over other Africans and at the same time trying to hold back the advance of whites. Whites were battling whites as British and Boers fought for control, while both fought the Africans. There was conflict between groups on all sides.

By 1900 it was not clear which group of whites would

win, but it was clear that the Africans had lost to superior technology. The military defeat by whites and loss of land did not turn the Africans into racists. White missionaries continued to operate in territories of African leaders such as Moshweshwe, Khama, Mzilikazi, and Dingane during all of their reigns, and friendly personal relationships were maintained between the races.

1900–1950

At the turn of the century, resistance against white domination took a new form. After 250 years of unsuccessful warfare, blacks resorted to techniques of petition, negotiation, and nonviolent direct action. Social action seldom fits neatly into time compartments, and there was overlap between the nineteenth and twentieth centuries as tactics were shifted. Mahatma Gandhi arrived in South Africa in 1893 and was soon involved in a petition campaign, South Africa's first, which resulted in ten thousand signatures protesting the removal of Asians from the voters' roll in Natal. The campaign was successful. In 1894, Gandhi founded the Natal Indian Congress to continue to press for Indian rights.

In a small military action in 1906, the Zulu rebellion led by Chief Bambata in Natal was quickly crushed. Gandhi recruited a medical unit of Indians to treat injured Zulus, a task refused by whites.

The beginnings of African nationalism and political organization, like the resistance of the Indian community, date back to the late nineteenth century. One African organization, Imbumba Yama Afrika, is sometimes called the seed of the African National Congress. It was formed in 1882 in the eastern Cape, where in 1884 the first African political newspaper was also started, with John Tengo Jabavu as editor. Early African political activity in the Cape was the result of the qualified franchise in that province. There were Africans able to meet the qualifications, which were economic rather than racial. Political activity of both Africans and coloureds tended to be an adjunct to white political activity.

The period between the Peace of Vereeniging in 1902, which ended the Anglo-Boer War, and the approval of Union in 1910, which established the current South African state, set the context within which most African political organization and activity germinated. There was a general dissatisfaction among blacks that the Peace of Vereeniging created no rights for them and failed to protect even the limited rights they already had.

Organizations which came into being at that time included the African Political Organization, the Transvaal National Natives Union, the Cape Native Congress, the Orange River Colony Native Congress, the Natal Native Congress, the Transvaal Native Vigilance Associations, the Transvaal British Indians Association, the Basuto Committee, the Native Congress (Transvaal), the Native Electoral Association, and the South African Native Convention.

Of these, the African Political Organization, with members in the Cape, Natal, and the Orange Free State, was the first national black resistance group. It was started by coloureds but also had African members.

Imvo Zabantsundu, Jabavu's newspaper, printed a petition to King Edward VII in 1905 from "the members of the Native United Political Association of the Transvaal Colony together with the natives of that Colony," protesting anti-African legislation.

At the time of the negotiations for the formation of the Union of South Africa, the South African Native Convention met to petition for "full and equal rights and privileges without distinction of class, colour or creed." The Convention's position went farther toward equality than the African Political Organization, which asked only for political rights for all "fully civilized" people. Neither petition was successful.

African nationalism in South Africa is often identified as beginning with the formation of the Union of South Africa in 1910. Blacks began then to seek a majority-rule state in opposition to white domination, although it would be many years before nationalism was articulated in that way.

With the failure to win rights in the agreement of Union and a general deteriorating political situation for blacks in all of the four provinces, the South African Native National Congress was founded in 1912. The name was changed to African National Congress in 1923. ANC is the oldest of all African liberation groups. Albert Luthuli, longtime ANC leader and a Nobel Peace Prize winner in 1960, said the business of ANC is "to right the total exclusion of the African from the management of South Africa, to give direction to the forces of liberation, to harness peacefully the growing resistance to continued oppression, and, by various nonviolent means, to demand the redress of injustice."

In today's context, when the South African government credits the Communists for every effort at black political advancement, it is important to see how much African effort and political organization was invested in the struggle for equality before the Communist Party was born. The resistance was expressed not only through 250 years of armed conflict but also through decades of organization. The Communist Party of South Africa was founded in 1921, and it made racial equality a major part of its agenda. However, the Communists were often openly critical of ANC, which would not add Communism to its own agenda.

Role of the Church

The main contribution of the church in the early days of the struggle against white domination is not in political and social action but rather in the education of the leaders and the members of African nationalist organizations. *The Oxford History of South Africa* reports that it was educated Christians, attracted to Western culture, who initiated the movement to African nationalism and shaped its ideology.[2]

At first only the church offered education to Africans.

Lovedale, one of the better-known missionary institutions, opened in 1841. By 1896, 3,448 African students had attended Lovedale. It was one of five or six mission schools in which the first African doctors, lawyers, editors, and political leaders received their education. Fort Hare, founded in 1916, was the first church-established college in all of southern Africa, attracting some of the political leaders of surrounding countries. Robert Mugabe and Simon Muzenda of Zimbabwe, for example, got their first higher education there. Joshua Nkomo attended another church-established school in South Africa, Adams College in Natal.

At the same time, church groups were sending Africans out of the country for higher education. The Natal Native Affairs Commissioner's report of 1906–7 estimated that at least 150 Africans were in the United States for study. There were probably more in Britain and a scattering in other countries. South African graduates come from a country four times the size of Zimbabwe, with an educational infrastructure that developed earlier and provided more national opportunities for higher education. A recent survey of personnel resources of Zimbabwe gave an estimate of 16,000 college graduates. South Africa clearly has many more black graduates than Zimbabwe. The memberships of ANC, PAC, the Black Consciousness Movement, and labor unions have grown beyond the pool of educated Christians. But the latter group still provides the major part of the leadership for resistance to white domination.

The first leadership in institutional separation from white domination also came from the church through the movement known as "Ethiopian churches." Some of these churches were established by the African Methodist Episcopal Church, a black-organized church in the United States. Other churches came from schisms within mission churches. The first Ethiopian church in South Africa was founded in 1892.

Help Sought Outside

At the turn of the century Africans were using a new technique of resistance: seeking political help from outside the country. Africans were successful in getting support from members of the British Parliament and others in the negotiations at the time of Union in 1910, but these British were as powerless in securing African rights as the Africans themselves were.

Delegations of Africans were sent to London in 1914 and again in 1919 to seek help from the Crown. Although those within the four provinces of South Africa received no help, Africans in Swaziland, Basutoland (now Lesotho), and Bechuanaland (now Botswana) were able to convince the Crown that they should not become part of South Africa. These three former protectorates are now independent countries.

At the beginning of the century, Indians led by Gandhi were also petitioning Britain for assistance in gaining their rights in South Africa. They asked for and received some help from India in pleading their cause, then and later. At that time Indian and African resistance and protest were separate, even when parallel action was underway.

After World War II the United Nations provided the structure for outside assistance against apartheid. From the beginning most of the nations of the world saw the protest against apartheid as a valid concern for the UN. By the late 1950s, the United States had conceded that racial discrimination in South Africa was an appropriate matter for UN consideration. After the Sharpeville Massacre in 1960, Britain finally joined the rest of the world in seeing apartheid as more than an internal matter for South Africa.

Mahatma Gandhi in South Africa

Mahatma Gandhi spent two periods of his life in South Africa. From 1893 to 1900 he led the petition campaign and organized the Natal Indian Congress. In 1901 he left South Africa to establish himself as a barrister in Bombay, but within a few months he received an urgent plea to return, this time to the Transvaal. He returned in early 1903.

The immediate problem to be confronted was an anti-Indian immigration law, but more threatening was a growing anti-Indian attitude on the part of Transvaal officialdom. Soon after his arrival, Gandhi said: "I could see that the Asiatic Department was merely a frightful engine of oppression for Indians."

The immigration law continued to be a matter of concern throughout Gandhi's time in South Africa, but the "Black Act," as the Indians called an Asian registration law proposed in 1906, soon took priority. This law called for registration and fingerprinting of all Asian men and women. Registration certificates would be required to obtain licenses to trade from the Transvaal. Failure to register would result in imprisonment. In an irony of colonial operations, the law was disallowed in 1906 by Britain, but when the Transvaal obtained responsible government status on January 1 of the following year, British approval of the legislation became automatic. In 1907 the Transvaal's first measure passed was the budget, the second was the Asiatic Registration Act.

Indian resentment of fingerprinting of women was so strong that women were exempted from registration, but the bill had no other changes from the original proposal. The Gandhi-led Indian response, first suggested by other Indian leaders, was a massive nonregistration campaign. It was within the context of this campaign that Gandhi coined the word *Satyagraha*. He rejected the term "passive resistance," although he approved "nonviolence" as an English equivalent. More specifically, Gandhi translated *Satyagraha* as "force which is truth and love" and also as "soul-force." Physical force, against either persons or property, was totally rejected.

Many were arrested for nonregistration, and Gandhi was among them. The campaign was called off when he thought he had worked out a compromise for voluntary registration and repeal of the law. When it became clear that General Smuts, then head of the Transvaal government, would not honor the agreement, the Indians held a mass protest, climaxed by a bonfire to destroy the voluntary certificates they had already obtained. The Indians wrote Smuts of their intent in advance; his response, as reported in the press, seems to have set the pattern for South African government leaders over the years: "I am sorry that some agitators are trying to inflame poor Indians who will be ruined if they succumb to their blandishments."

The Transvaal also passed a discriminatory immigration law in 1907 and jailed and deported Indians for refusing to comply with the registration and immigration laws. Some Indians, imprisoned in the Diepkloof Convict Prison with a jailor who insulted them, pioneered with a hunger strike. After seven days they were transferred to another prison, an alternative they said would be acceptable if the objectionable jailor was not removed from Diepkloof.

On March 14, 1913, a judge in the Cape Supreme Court ruled that the only legal marriages in South Africa were those performed by the Christian rites and registered by the Registrar of Marriages. This invalidated most Indian marriages, as few Indians were Christians. Gandhi's effort to get legislative relief was unsuccessful. *Satyagrahis* for the first time included women who entered the Transvaal illegally and sold goods on the streets without a license, seeking arrest to protest the nullification of their marriages. At first the women were not arrested, but by September and October groups of both men and women, who would leave the territory and then reenter illegally, were arrested and sentenced to three months in prison. Meanwhile, a head tax on some Indian laborers was added to the list of grievances.

The final protest was a march by Gandhi of 1,037 men, 127 women, and 57 children into the Transvaal from Natal. They started out on November 6, 1913, and twice en route Gandhi was arrested and released on bond. On a third arrest he was sentenced to jail for nine months. The marchers were deported to Natal in three trains. In Natal they were sent to jail, then moved to a coal mine, where they refused to work. Not surprisingly, supporting strikes developed among other Indian workers.

In the course of negotiations with Smuts, all issues were eventually settled to the satisfaction of the Indians. Gandhi then felt free to return to India in July 1914. He wrote: "Our victory was implicit in our combination of the two qualities of nonviolence and determination."

As Gandhi's work drew the attention of Africans, cooperation began between the Natal Indian Congress and ANC. His work in South Africa is, however, primarily of historical interest, for it was here that he worked through some of his ideas and tested them successfully in a few limited campaigns. Ironically, it is Gandhi's work in India which had significant impact on the thinking of African leaders. Albert Luthuli became a convert to Gandhi's methods. Other African leaders—such as Kenneth Kaunda, now President of Zambia; Chief Gatsha Buthelezi, head of Inkatha and KwaZulu; and Robert Mugabe, Prime Minister of Zimbabwe—acknowledge Gandhi's influence on their ideas, as did Robert Sobukwe, founder of the Pan Africanist Congress, and Steve Biko, leader of the Black Consciousness Movement.

Other Pre-1950 Resistance

Africans organized and led numerous nonviolent actions of resistance in the period before 1950. In 1913, for example, African women in the Orange Free State averted the extension of pass laws to them by refusing to carry passes. In 1943, a bus boycott in the African township of Alexandra was provoked by a fare increase, nineteen years before the Montgomery, Alabama, boycott.

A 1919 ANC anti-pass campaign resulted in 500 arrests in Johannesburg. Also in that city, among the first strikes in

South Africa were those of African sanitation workers in 1918. Four hundred dockers struck in Cape Town in 1919, and some 40,000 African miners struck in 1920.

Three Africans were killed by police in a pass-burning demonstration in 1930. African women organized nonviolent resistance in 1932 against curfew regulations in the Transvaal.

In 1943, the most massive African strike included over 70,000 mine workers, nine of whom were killed by police. Another strike in 1946 was broken by police.

The Indians remembered some of Gandhi's lessons. Six hundred Indians were jailed in Natal in 1944 for their resistance against segregation. Nearly 2,000 Indians (and a few whites, including Rev. Michael Scott) were jailed in Natal for nonviolent resistance to anti-Indian legislation. Blacks continued organizing and promoting political action, in addition to demonstrations. The nationwide South African Indian Congress was formed in 1926. Impatient with their elders, younger members of ANC formed the Congress Youth League in 1944.

After World War II, Dr. A. B. Xuma, ANC leader, published a popular book, *African Claims,* in which he applied the ideals of the Atlantic Charter to South Africa.

For South African blacks, the first half of the twentieth century was a time of facing up to the reality of white domination. Laws were getting more restrictive against all blacks. At the same time, there was some hope that organization, petition, goodwill, and logic might make some inroads on the obvious injustices.

1950–1975

The third quarter of the twentieth century brought increasing oppression, with the government using more and more force to maintain the status quo. It was also a time of mounting resistance by blacks. When the Group Areas Act was passed in 1950, ANC sponsored a mass labor strike in

Transvaal townships. Police opened fire on a crowd of protesters, killing eighteen and wounding thirty.

The first nationwide campaign of resistance, the Defiance
Against Unjust Laws Campaign, was planned in 1951 and
launched in 1952 with remarkable success during its first four
months. The campaign was organized by ANC, with the
Indian Congress participating. Its leaders had developed a
nonviolent strategy which would dramatize the injustice of
the laws by accepting arrest for violating those laws. The
authorities would be notified of the time and place of each
act of civil disobedience. In the whole campaign more than
8,000 persons were arrested, among them Gandhi's son and
a few whites. Crowds of over 10,000 attended open-air
meetings at Cape Town, Port Elizabeth, East London, Pretoria, and Durban on June 26, 1952, and for the first time,
the white press gave almost daily coverage to the campaign.
ANC membership increased from 7,000 to 100,000. Although Nelson Mandela was the key figure in the implementation of this campaign, Albert Luthuli was nominally
in charge of the operation, and the government Native Affairs Department deposed him from his chieftainship because of it. Eventually, Luthuli was restricted to his home
village.

After four months of highly disciplined nonviolent action, rioting broke out in Port Elizabeth, Johannesburg,
Kimberley, and East London. At least forty persons were
killed, and there was extensive property damage. The riots
ended the Defiance Campaign. Luthuli and ANC charged
that agents provocateurs were responsible for starting the
riots, an accusation with which most informed foreign observers agree. In his autobiography Luthuli concludes: "The
prospect before the white supremacists, if they were going
to react to our challenge in a civilized way, was that arrests
would continue indefinitely. Behind the thousands already
arrested there were more, many more. The challenge of
nonviolence was more than they could meet. It robbed them
of the initiative." Therefore, Luthuli reports, violence was

initiated by the police to create the riots and restore initiative to whites.

Resistance Spreads

In spite of its untimely and unfortunate end, the Defiance Campaign served notice on South African whites that African resistance had to be taken seriously. After the campaign, Julius Lewin, a noted South African lecturer on African law, pointed out that "the first effect of undermining Congress was to strengthen those less responsible and less reasonable groups in African life that have begun to preach enmity against all white people as such, and perhaps to toy with the idea of terrorism as a technique for securing political change."[3] Lewin was right, missing only the point that it would be the African National Congress itself that would feel forced to undertake that kind of action which its opponents called terrorism. Lewin (a man his fellow white South Africans should have taken more seriously) also pointed out that for South African government "there are no moderate African leaders." The real leaders were already at a more radical level than was acceptable to the government.

The Defiance Campaign ended, but resistance continued, with many sponsors in addition to the ANC. As Luthuli reported: "Throughout the country as a whole resistance was uncoordinated and haphazard. But it was there, and it arose out of the whites' refusal to share the country with us, or to permit us to walk free in our own land."

Resistance has always been varied and sometimes haphazard in South Africa. There are many, many examples to report.

In Namibia in 1924, a hundred Khoikhoi were killed in the course of refusing to pay a dog tax.

In the first of many protests against the Bantu Education Act of 1953, a school boycott sponsored by ANC in 1955 resulted in 100,000 students staying home.

In 1956, thousands of African women took to the streets

protesting the extension of pass laws to women. The police responded with force. Three women were killed.

In 1955, the vision of an egalitarian South Africa was articulated by representatives of all races in the adoption of the Freedom Charter by 3,000 delegates meeting in an open field at Kliptown. The Freedom Charter, still a basic manifesto for ANC, declares that South Africa belongs to all of its people. "Every man and woman shall have the right to vote for and stand as candidate for all bodies which make laws." As a cooperative effort by ANC, the Congress of Democrats, and a number of other groups, the adoption of the Freedom Charter was a high point in the life of the soon to decline Congress Alliance.

We, the people of South Africa, declare for all our country and the world to know: that South Africa belongs to all who live in it, black and white, and that no government can justly claim authority unless it is based on the will of all the people; that our people have been robbed of their birthright to land, liberty and peace by a form of government founded on injustice and inequality; that our country will never be prosperous or free until all our people live in brotherhood, enjoying equal rights and opportunities; that only a democratic state, based on the will of all the people, can secure to all their birthright without distinction of colour, race, sex or belief. . . .
—from the Freedom Charter of South Africa [4]

Robert Sobukwe broke with ANC in 1958 to organize the Pan Africanist Congress (PAC), a new liberation group emphasizing black unity and leadership. PAC provided a new focal point for resistance. The first big action by PAC was a nonviolent demonstration against passes in 1960. What has come to be known as the Sharpeville Massacre was one result, with 70 Africans killed and 186 wounded by South African forces. Many were shot in the back as they fled from the scene. In the following three weeks there were massive demonstrations, marches, gatherings, and pass burnings across the country. There were thousands of arrests, and the South African government passed its 90-day detention law as a new repressive measure.

Black Attitudes Begin to Change

Sharpeville marks a clear transition point in the attitude of South African blacks on the tactics of liberation. There had long been a division between those committed solely to nonviolent action and those who thought nonviolence was not enough by itself. After Sharpeville, there was an almost unanimous coming together to the view that violence is necessary to win liberation for South African blacks.

Late in 1961 ANC members, including some members of the Communist Party, formed Umkonto We Sizwe ("Spear of the Nation" in Zulu) to carry out sabotage. The group included Africans, Indians, and whites. December 16 is the Day of the Covenant, a "holy day" in South Africa for Afrikaners commemorating the victory at Blood River. On that day in 1961 the group placed bombs in Johannesburg and Port Elizabeth aimed at destroying property, not persons. In the following eighteen months until they were captured, they claimed more than seventy acts of sabotage. Sabotage under the name Spear of the Nation continues.

A short-lived violent, anti-white creation of PAC in the early 1960s called "Poqo" (Xhosa for "alone") was crushed and most of its known leaders executed. Poqo was the forerunner of APLA (Azanian People's Liberation Army), another creation of PAC.

In spite of the acceptance of violence as necessary by many Africans, liberation leaders agree that nonviolence is a satisfactory complement to violent protest or guerrilla warfare.

In 1961, the year after Sharpeville, ANC attempted to organize a three-day nationwide strike in protest of a "white only" referendum. The government countered with massive action, and the strike had only limited success.

Black Consciousness

In 1969 the South Africa Students' Organization (SASO) split from the nonracial but white-led National Union of South African Students (NUSAS) and from the University Christian Movement. The President of SASO was Steve Biko, who believed that Africans must provide their own leadership for liberation. Even though NUSAS was already seen by the government as a subversive organization, Biko did not feel that NUSAS could meet the need of blacks. SASO quickly won African, coloured, and Indian student support. Marxists were critical of SASO for, as they saw it, failing to understand the class struggle.

In 1970, Biko became a leading exponent of the Black Consciousness Movement for promoting the SASO idea of black leadership, much like the Black Power movement in the United States. Related organizations included the Black People's Convention (BPC). BPC immediately ruled out all cooperation with homeland leaders and government institutions. Black Community Programs (BCP) was supported by the South African Council of Churches and the Christian Institute. High school and primary students formed the South African Student Movement (SASM) in Soweto, and similar groups were organized elsewhere.

In September 1974, SASO and BPC defied a ban and held a "Viva FRELIMO" rally in Durban and at the University of the North to celebrate the liberation of Mozambique. Many blacks were arrested at both rallies, and nine leaders were charged. Over the two years of their trial the defendants often entered the courtroom singing freedom songs or giving the Black Power salute and shout. The news media kept the public informed during the trial. The defendants were finally given five- and six-year sentences.

In December 1974, the Black Renaissance Convention met. More than 300 African, coloured, and Asian participants were brought together by Catholic and Protestant leaders. This group of intellectuals, considered moderate, discussed Black Consciousness ideas. The convention called for a united, democratic South Africa with one person, one vote and an equitable distribution of wealth. It also called for foreign countries to withdraw cultural, educational, and economic support from "the existing racist government and all its racist institutions."

A major impact on resistance in 1971 was the strike of African workers in Namibia. Most whites thought that these mostly illiterate workers were incapable of organizing. The strike, however, was widespread and brought some improvement for the workers. Their action encouraged other strikes and was probably a factor in the government's overhaul of labor laws.

Black dockworkers followed with a strike in Durban in 1972. Fifteen workers lost their jobs, but a pay increase was won. The next year there were strikes in Durban, Cape Town, and Hammersdale, with mixed results. But black labor was moving to the forefront as another power for resistance. All these strikes of the early 1970s were illegal, but at the time the government seemed unable to deal with strikes by its usual law-and-order methods.

1975–1980

The years since 1975 have been filled with black resistance and government response. Sharpeville, the rash of strikes, and the Black Consciousness Movement set the context for the Soweto rebellion and its aftermath.

A youth crusade shook South Africa as the 1976 Soweto demonstration grew into the third nationwide protest action. On June 16, 1976, 20,000 students in Soweto, an African township with a population of nearly two million, started a peaceful march toward a protest meeting to be held in Orlando Stadium. The protest was organized to object to a long-standing but newly enforced government ruling that one-half of all high school subjects were to be taught in Afrikaans instead of English. The South Africa Student Movement (SASM) had organized the meeting. The students were in good spirits and carried signs indicating the nonviolent nature of the protest. Before they reached the stadium they were confronted by police. It is unclear whether the students threw stones first or the police fired first, but the police fired into the unarmed crowd of youngsters. The first to be killed was a thirteen-year-old boy, Hector Petersen. The picture of him being carried out of the action has become a powerful symbol of the Soweto uprising.

The Bantu Education Act had already been the object of sporadic protest since its inception in 1953. Afrikaans, the language of white officials and those considered to be the primary oppressors, was considered to be the language of oppression. Students had been highly politicized by the Black Consciousness Movement, and police action in Soweto was the spark that set off nationwide protest. Before the protests were over, between 700 and 1,000 persons were killed, including 50 coloureds. More than 5,000 were injured. Two whites were beaten to death in Soweto on the first day of the rebellion. There were other isolated white deaths, but their number remained small, probably not more than six in all. The cost of white supremacy is typically paid in black corpses.

Many post-Soweto demonstrations were nonviolent, but there was also widespread destruction of government property in African townships. Soweto hardened the belief of black students (and adults as well) that violence is necessary to end South African oppression. An estimated 10,000 students left the country for guerrilla training or education as a result of Soweto.

In addition to hardening black attitudes on the use of violence, Soweto and its aftermath shifted the focus of resistance to a younger generation and more dispersed leadership. Some leaders from the older generation had to run rapidly to catch up with those they thought they led. Protests by youth in South Africa have never completely ceased since 1976. There were widespread school boycotts again in 1980 and 1981 involving blacks, coloureds, and Asians.

The death of Steve Biko while in police custody (see Chapter 1) touched off wide protests in 1977. Again, the ground had been well prepared by events, for in addition to consciousness raising by the Black Consciousness Movement, Steve Biko's violent death was the forty-fourth death of a political prisoner in police custody within fifteen years. Some of these prisoners "jumped" out of windows; some were found hanging in their cells; some were listed "cause of death unknown."

The protest against Steve Biko's death brought a heavy-handed response from the South African government. Seventeen Black Consciousness organizations and the Christian Institute were banned. The *World,* a white-owned, black-edited newspaper, was closed down. Percy Qoboza, editor of the *World,* and Dr. Nthato Motlana, chairman of the Committee of Ten, a Soweto leadership group which emerged from the Soweto rebellion, were detained. Seven whites well known for their work for racial equality were banned, including two Afrikaners, Beyers Naudé, founder of the Christian Institute, and Theo Kotze, Director of the Institute in Cape Town. Donald Woods, editor of the East London *Daily Dispatch,* was also banned. Kotze and Woods left South Africa, and Beyers Naudé, no longer banned, now serves as General Secretary of the South African Council of Churches.

Some indication of the continued tempo of resistance in the 1970s is indicated by the following table:

*Prosecutions from July 1, 1978, to June 30, 1979,
under the Internal Security Act*[5]

Public violence	1,130
Unlawful and riotous assembly	253
Sabotage	86
Intent to racial unrest	23
Malicious damage to property	16,283
Arson	1,059
Obstructing	221
Total	19,055

If a proportionate number of U.S. citizens were prosecuted for security violations, it would mean nearly 200,000 prosecutions per year.

4

Repression, Resistance, Response

—To uphold Christian values and civilised norms,
with recognition and protection of freedom of
faith and worship
—To safeguard the integrity and freedom of our
country
—To uphold the independence of the judiciary, and
the equality of all under the law
—To secure the maintenance of law and order
—To further the contentment and spiritual and
material welfare of all
—To respect and protect the human dignity, life,
liberty and property of all in our midst
—To respect, to further and to protect the self-
determination of population groups and peoples
—To promote private initiative and effective
competition

> —From the Preamble to the 1983
> South Africa Constitution

The attempt in this chapter is not to detail and document
the increase in repression and resistance, coupled with government response to change, but to give some overview of
the nature of developments, the direction in which they are
moving, and to indicate the role of various participants.

South Africa was deceptively quiet in 1980. The South
African government and representatives of American business were assuring everyone that everything was normal and

it was a great time for tourism and foreign investment. Incidents of unrest seemed sporadic and scattered. They received almost no attention in United States and little press attention in South Africa. Yet, for that year, all outdoor meetings were banned except for sporting events, and as documented in the first edition of *Challenge and Hope,* there were 65 serious incidents with arrests, tear gas, police gunfire, stonings, etc. There were 207 "illegal job actions" (strikes by Africans) and 32 security trials (pp. 63–70). Subsequent information indicates that the *Challenge and Hope* numbers were low.

The protest actions picked up rapidly. In just the category of political violence and sabotage, incidents rose from 59 in 1980 to 395 in 1983. Fatalities in these incidents rose from 39 in 1980 to 214 in 1983. Nonfatal injuries were 59 in 1980 and 815 in 1983.[1] These were only the guerrilla action cases. There were many more school boycotts, protest marches, and other action. Violence was also rampant in the homelands. Between July and September of 1983 there were 90 people killed in the Ciskei by the police in response to a bus boycott.[2] By 1983, word was reaching tourists. In an extreme example, tourists from Argentina dropped from over 200,000 in 1979 to fewer than 2,000 in 1983.[3]

As reported in Chapter 3, sporadic and often massive black resistance goes back almost to the time of the first settlement at the Cape. However, in every instance of intensified resistance—from the Zulu wars to Gandhi's campaign with the Indians through the Sharpeville Massacre in 1960—the government regained control, and resistance seethed beneath the surface until it broke through again at some other place, over different issues and with new participants. Between the outbreaks of organized resistance there was a superficial, false impression of peace widely hailed by the promoters of the status quo.

The growing resistance of the early 1980s started with the Soweto uprising in 1976. In spite of, or perhaps even because of, the violent repression of the Soweto demonstration and the oppressive measures which followed, the South African government has never gained complete control of the resistance movement since the Soweto uprising. Hundreds of young people left the country hoping to infiltrate back again as trained guerrilla fighters. It was at Soweto that the resistance became a youth movement. Black education, the issue at the Soweto demonstration, became the issue across the country, with school boycotts widespread. When the resistance became a youth issue, the students were freed from school to be troops of the resistance with their energy, enthusiasm, and rash fearlessness. Resistance spread: school boycotts increased, Soweto was commemorated annually, there were rent and bus boycotts, there was new labor action, and increased guerrilla activity by the liberation movements. World protests became louder.

It was within the post-Soweto social dynamics that the grim pattern of repression, resistance, and response developed. The supporters of the status quo lost their grip, and were devoid of the ability needed to deal with the problems. The response of government was sometimes increased oppression with declarations of emergency, new and harsher laws, and massive detentions. Sometimes the government response was an increment of change. As the resisters saw it, there was not much difference between the oppression and the change.

The year 1983 has already been noted as a time of greatly increased resistance. The government fueled resistance in 1983 with a major change, the tricameral legislature. With a separate section for whites, coloureds, and Indians, the legislature is still under the control of whites. The new Parliament continues institutionalized racism. This proposal to the Parliament session of 1983 was approved by a white voters' referendum on November 2 of that year, and the new Parliament opened September 18, 1984.

This beginning of national power sharing with Asians and coloureds was opposed by Africans, most coloureds and Asians, far-right whites, and some liberal whites. Liberal whites split, some welcoming the new Parliament as a first step in giving political opportunity to blacks. The President's Council, a part of the new constitution, has 60 members, 20 of whom are nominated by the white legislators and 25 named by the State President. Among its duties is to settle differences among the three chambers. In June 1986, when the white chamber voted for increasing the time people could be held in detention without charges and the Asian and coloured chambers voted against the bill, the President's Council voted for the bill. The Parliament is sexist as well as racist. There are 38 members and deputy members in the cabinet and the ministerial councils; none is a woman.

United Democratic Front

If the new constitution had included a fourth chamber for Africans, the majority of Africans probably would have opposed participation in it, as did the majority of coloureds and Indians. However, the exclusion of Africans from the beginning of power sharing was a powerful stimulus to resistance.

Growing out of the resistance to the new Parliament was the United Democratic Front (UDF), an amazing accomplishment of organization. UDF was founded on August 20, 1983, at a meeting of about 1,000 delegates representing 575 organizations. About 650 organizations, with perhaps two million members, eventually affiliated. Although largely black, UDF is nonracial in its membership.

The government sees UDF as its most powerful anti-apartheid foe within the country. A few of the UDF leaders have been murdered and over half its leaders arrested. Some were charged with treason, although the charges were eventually dropped. UDF has been able to continue vigorous opposition to apartheid and maintain its legal status. UDF is committed to nonviolent methods of struggle.

On October 9, 1986, the South African government declared UDF to be an "affected organization." This does not ban the UDF, but it prohibits it from receiving any financial support from outside of South Africa.

Resistance Increases

The opening of the new Parliament with its new pattern of white political domination coincided with a new phase of resistance. UDF became the focal point of resistance and government repression, although the activity of black trade unions increased and there were numerous civic organizations battling apartheid, particularly on local issues. The churches became more forceful, with clergy speaking out from the pulpit and at the funerals of protesters and innocent bystanders killed by police action. In addition to these more formal protests, the "comrades," young blacks in townships, increased their forays of stoning police patrols and killing and harassing "collaborators."

On July 21, 1985, the government declared a state of emergency in most of the main population areas of the country and it was continued until March 7, 1986. The declaration provided a justification for thousands of arrests and detentions. An estimated 86 percent of the arrests in the first two weeks during the state of emergency were of leaders of UDF or its affiliated organizations. African townships were heavily patrolled by the armed forces as well as the police. Like an army of occupation, 35,000 troops patrolled 96 African townships in 1985. When two people met they could be charged as an illegal gathering. Hundreds of children were arrested, sometimes in schoolrooms and sometimes for not being in school. The Lawyers Committee on Human Rights in New York reports that more than 2,000 children under the age of sixteen were detained for some of the time from July 1985 until March 1986. The imposition of the state of emergency had little effect on resistance or lowering the death rate resulting from the resistance.

In early May [1986] police broke into Arcadia High
School in Bronteheuwel after coloured pupils had
been involved in a demonstration, and whipped
their victims with sjamboks [leather whips]. The
School Committee reported that the police seemed
to take "particular pleasure to damage the faces of
the pupils" and that "children had to drag themselves between two rows of policemen as the
sjambok blows rained down on them." Five were
hospitalised, a number scarred for life and one reportedly faced the likelihood of losing an eye. In
all, two pupils were charged with "public violence" but released two days later without any al-
legation against them. Indeed, we heard, with de-
pressing repetition, accounts of violence directed
by the security forces against children, of children
brutally whipped, of schoolrooms tear-gassed and
of difficulties experienced by parents in locating
children taken by police.
        —*Mission to South Africa: The Commonwealth
        Report*[4]

On June 12, 1986, the government declared a new, nationwide state of emergency four days before the tenth anniversary of the Soweto uprising. It was the first nationwide
state of emergency since the Sharpeville Massacre. It resulted in the detention of thousands, banned all meetings
except regular indoor church services, and placed heavy restrictions on the press. Under the government's show of
force, June 16 passed relatively quietly but with tremendous
absenteeism from work and school and a few courageous,
illegal commemorations in churches.

Five days after the observance, which was supposedly the
cause for the new state of emergency, the police authorities
announced new restrictions around Cape Town for 119

groups. Included were UDF, the Congress of South African Trade Unions, the Azanian African People's Organization, the End Conscription Campaign, and the Detainees' Parents Support Committee. The organizations were prohibited from publishing pamphlets or posters, and their officials could not be quoted in the media. A month later these restrictions were withdrawn, at least temporarily, after a South African Supreme Court ruling that the order was issued by an unauthorized official. State President P. W. Botha then issued a decree granting the officials proper authority to act without court interference.

The cost of all of this repression and resistance in lives, detentions, and economic terms is difficult to document. South Africa confirms few detentions and prohibits publication of the names of detainees in the press. In June 1986, when the government had confirmed the names of only 30 detainees, the Detainees' Parents Support Committee had a list of 1,034 missing persons.[5] This list was thought to represent perhaps one-third of the detainees at that time. However, a subsequent government report named 8,501 detainees. Police reports on the number of deaths are unreliable and nearly always lower than the grim body count. The Commonwealth Group (see Chapter 6) reported that in a case where the police reported 24 deaths a father searching for his son counted 40 bodies in a morgue; other morgues were also in use.

It would be reasonable to estimate that from September 1984 to August 1, 1986, 2,000 persons were killed and 19,000 arrested or detained. Detainees may be held six months without trial or even access to their families or lawyers. Most, but not all, of these victims of apartheid were black.

One of the higher costs of the repression and resistance, both now and to be carried far into the future, is that being paid by youth. Lost educational opportunities alone are staggering. After a brief period when school boycotts were ended in early 1986, school boycotts by students and school closings by the government began again. The government is not releasing statistics on school closings, although it was announced in September 1986 that 33 schools were closed in the Eastern Cape and an undisclosed number were closed in the Johannesburg area. Probably thousands of black students at the high school level had no option for school attendance for much of the 1986 school year and little hope for the next year.

Further, youth are participating in the violence of the resistance and repression and are being traumatized by the entire experience, irrespective of the degree of participation by any particular young person. Estimates run as high as 40 percent of detainees being under the age of eighteen.

The longer the states of emergency continue, the higher the cost to everyone. The polarization of the South African society magnified by the emergency leaves moderates, black and white, little opportunity for effective action.

By October 1986, press reports in the United States indicated that the level of violence in South Africa was in steep decline from earlier in the year. The South African government maintained that the country was enjoying greatly increased stability with only isolated incidents of "unrest." This "stability," however, is an illusion created by the nearly total ban on TV coverage, the heavy restrictions placed on the rest of the press, and the high concentration of security forces in black areas.

The state-controlled television and radio news service produces nothing about the crisis here except government propaganda, quoting people out of context, omitting major news items, exaggerating other information . . . whatever will promote the position of the state. The only news on unrest or the action of police and the military comes from the Minister of Information. All else is prohibited under penalty of prosecution or deportation. And this week it was confirmed by the state

that the State of Emergency will not soon end. I am having this letter mailed from Europe by a current visitor to this country because I don't trust that it will get out of South Africa otherwise.
—from a letter dated June 26, 1986, from a church worker who obviously cannot be named

Change in Response to Resistance

In addition to heavy repression, the South African government also offered a carrot, abolition of the hated pass laws. Enforcement of the applicable laws was stopped in April 1986, and those in prison for pass law offenses were released. The laws were subsequently repealed. In place of the pass, Africans, and all other citizens, will have to carry identity cards. It may take years to get the cards produced and distributed. The effect of this change is difficult to foretell, but the release of people from prison is to be welcomed, and if the more than 100,000 persons per year arrested for pass law offenses don't get arrested for identity card offenses, it will bring about a marked improvement.

Another positive response by the government was the publication* of legislation in May 1986 extending the right of freehold property rights to Africans. Previously, only 99-year leaseholds were available to them.

A third response came under the guise of power sharing: the creation of the National Council, an advisory body of Africans and others, to draw up a new constitution. This move clearly makes little difference. Few, if any, Africans with suitable leadership qualifications will participate.

Blacks also eased their pressure on the government a bit by ending, for the time being, the school boycott. The decision was made by a conference called by the National Ed-

---

*The time of "publication of legislation" in South Africa is the point at which new legislation goes into effect.

ucation Crisis Committee. The conference, with more than 1,000 delegates, met in Durban in April 1986. The conference survived considerable harassment by Inkatha, the Zulu political and cultural organization. Inkatha was formally condemned by the conference as an "enemy of the people" and a "fascist organization in league with the government." Chief Buthelezi denied that Inkatha had organized the attacks against the conference.

Uncoordinated school boycotts soon began again over the issue of Army personnel in uniform being assigned to school grounds for "security" reasons.

Judgments on Change

The impact of governmental change in South Africa is often quite different from what the government expects. Power sharing in the tricameral Parliament, which was publicized to the world, turned out to be a dud from the very beginning. The effect was greatly heightened resistance.

How can one assess the potential for real change in any announced action by the South African government or others? Concerned citizens opposed to apartheid may have difficulty in judging the value of any particular change.

A few questions provide guidelines for assessing change. Negative answers flash a warning.

1. Does the change alter basic power relationships?

2. Are blacks who are respected and supported by the majority of the people involved in initiating and planning the change?

3. Do diverse groups inside and outside South Africa voice approval of the change?

4. Are costs paid primarily by those in power and benefits accrued primarily to those without power?

5. Are appropriate means for implementation announced and followed?

6. Is there a timetable for swift, visible achievement of goals?

From the answers to these questions it becomes clear that while some reforms announced by the government may be positive in themselves, they do not represent fundamental change in apartheid.

The Church

The church has taken an increasing role in resistance in South Africa. Allan Boesak, President of the World Alliance of Reformed Churches, who is a local pastor in South Africa and one of the founders of the UDF; Bishop Desmond Tutu, Archbishop of Cape Town and Metropolitan of the Church of the Province of Southern Africa; and Beyers Naudé, General Secretary of the South African Council of Churches, have outstanding, courageous records of public leadership against apartheid. They are the better known but are only three of a great many church leaders in the struggle for liberation based on theological justification.

Differences in theology, leadership, and history make it difficult to generalize about the church. There are three branches of the Dutch Reformed Church, in addition to their "sister churches" of races other than white. The Dutch Reformed is the traditional church of the Afrikaners. The Roman Catholic and Anglican churches are strong and often in the forefront of the anti-apartheid struggle. In addition to the mainstream Protestant denominations, both theologically right-wing and left-wing, there are about 4,000 African independent churches. A few of these have a membership in the thousands, but many are single churches under a strong leader. The total membership of the independent churches has been estimated to be as high as eight million. These churches tend to be apolitical, but many of their members are active in trade unions, civic organizations, and groups associated with UDF.

The Nederduitsch Hervormde Kerk (NHK), one of the three Dutch Reformed churches, reaffirmed its whites-only membership as recently as May 1986. The other two DRCs have abandoned that policy and were sharply critical of the NHK decision. Allan Boesak, a pastor in the coloured division of the DRC, points out that his part of the DRC has declared apartheid to be a heresy. After that, he says, "there is nothing more to be said about the system—all that is left is action."[6] The DRC originally gave biblical support for apartheid. Boesak calls the change "the struggle for the integrity of the gospel."

The three originally all-white DRC churches do not belong to the South Africa Council of Churches, although the black DRC churches do. SACC has taken the lead in organized church resistance. At its national conference in 1985, SACC supported disinvestment and called on "member churches and individual Christians to withdraw participation in the economic system that oppresses the poor, by reinvesting money and energy in alternative economic systems in existence in our region." SACC, like the Southern African Catholic Bishops' Conference, has supported the right of conscientious objection to conscription into the South African Defence Force.

The Kairos Document, *Challenge to the Church: A Theological Comment on the Political Crisis in South Africa,* breaks new ground in an attack by the church on South African government policies. Issued in September 1985, it grew out of extensive discussions by theologians and church leaders. It was signed by 151 church leaders, white as well as black, by the time of publication, and more signers are adding their names. Included among the signers were representatives of normally apolitical churches such as the Assemblies of God, the Order of the Ethiopian Church, the United Independent Believers of Christ, and the Ebenezer Evangelical Church. These churches are not customarily expected to make a radical political statement. Excerpts from the Kairos Document are printed in the Appendix.

Divergence of the positions of the church in South Africa and the government goes back as far as 1953, when the government took over black education in order to impose Bantu

Education on all Africans. Previous to 1953, nearly all of the education of Africans in the rural areas was done by missionaries with more liberal attitudes on race than the National Party government.

Church efforts in the growing resistance of the 1980s include Days of Prayer to End Unjust Rule, refusal to participate in the celebration of national holidays commemorating military victories over Africans, consumer boycotts, marches and other demonstrations calling for freeing political prisoners, civil disobedience by carrying out religious funerals for victims of police action, mixed-race services in proscribed areas, support for conscientious objectors to conscription, and legal and financial aid for victims of government repression.

The Christian church can no longer be counted on by the government to support official policy. It is a force for radical, humane change for building a democratic society based on justice. The church will probably be one of the few institutions in the current struggle to provide centers for compassion and stability in the much more difficult days ahead.

Anti-conscription Resistance

Churches have been in the lead in resisting conscription and supporting objectors. Resistance to conscription in South Africa takes on an unusually important role. Advocacy of conscientious objection is a crime. Military duty is compulsory for all white males for up to four years of their lives spread out over a long period of time; it is the point at which young men are asked to support apartheid directly. Until 1983, there were no statutory provisions for conscientious objection. Religious objection is now recognized. Those assigned to alternative civilian service must serve one and a half times the length of conscripted military duty. Since military duty is staggered over a number of years, it still is unclear what time the conscientious objector must serve, but it is a maximum of six years.

Up to February 1986, 657 men had applied for C.O. status, and only 12 were denied.[7] More than two-thirds of the applicants were Jehovah's Witnesses.

The End Conscription Campaign is the main organization trying to stop conscription and to support objectors, including those who do not claim to act out of religious faith. ECC is highly suspect to the government, and many of its leaders have been detained. The conscription picture is much like that in the United States during the Vietnam War. Many objectors "vote with their feet," i.e., leave the country. It is estimated that as many as 10,000 draft-age men have left South Africa. Many others attempt to evade the law by going underground. As with conscientious objector service, the penalty for breaking the conscription law is to spend one and a half times the period of prescribed military duty, and it must be served in prison.

Refusal to accept conscription is a growing edge of white resistance to apartheid. There were 1,600 "no shows" in all of 1984. The End Conscription Campaign reported that 7,589 young white men failed to show up when called in January 1985. The South African government has refused to release information on the number of men who failed to report in January 1986.

Liberation Movements

The South African government faces the opposition of three liberation movement organizations: the South West African People's Organization (SWAPO), the African National Congress (ANC), and the Pan Africanist Congress (PAC).

SWAPO relates only to Namibia, and ANC and PAC to South Africa, although they support each other's struggle. SWAPO is clearly the chief opposition to South Africa in Namibia, although there are many small organizations offering various degrees of resistance within Namibia. SWAPO is recognized by the UN as the sole representative of the Namibian people. It is SWAPO that is carrying on the civil war in northern Namibia, and it is there that South Africa and SWAPO confront one another militarily. Both SWAPO and South Africa have accepted in principle that Namibia should obtain its freedom through a UN-supervised election to establish an independent government.

ANC, the ancestor of all African liberation movements, was founded in 1912. Much of its history is reported in Chapter 3. ANC is recognized as the primary liberation movement by most groups. It has come to greater prominence during 1985–86 as South African business groups and others, over the protests of the South African government, have gone to ANC headquarters in Lusaka for dialogue. Winnie Mandela's public role in South Africa and the campaign to free Nelson Mandela from prison have added to the image of the ANC. ANC is credited with most of the guerrilla warfare activity in South Africa, although it (as well as the other groups) makes no claims about the many incidents of sabotage. Both ANC and PAC are outlawed in South Africa, but this has not stopped frequent displays of support for ANC.

PAC was created as a result of a Black Consciousness split from ANC in 1959. It has gone through a long period of internal dissension and reorganization. PAC has not been in the news much during the growing resistance of the 1980s, and that tends to underrate its influence. There are strong Black Consciousness currents within South Africa. The Azanian African People's Organization (AZAPO) is legal within South Africa and active as the largest Black Consciousness group. The National Forum is an association of Black Consciousness groups. The Black Consciousness groups tend to give hesitant support or are in opposition to activities by UDF and its groups. As it is assumed that UDF is in the ANC camp (loosely compatible, not organizationally tied or committed), it is assumed that the National Forum is in the PAC camp.

Neither ANC nor PAC claim responsibility for the massive resistance within the African townships during the 1980s, although ANC supporters have been greatly in evidence. The South African government calls all members of liberation movements "terrorists." It gives credit for liberation leadership to Communists. This narrow and erroneous perspective is a major hurdle in moving the South African struggle into meaningful dialogue for settlement.

Black vs. Black

The 1980s have seen a large increase in what the South African government calls "black-on-black" violence. The term conceals the nature of that violence and particularly conceals the fact that the majority of the black-on-black killings have been committed by government surrogates.

There are at least three distinct categories of black-on-black violence:

1. "Official" blacks commit "official" violence. Police officers of the South African government, the self-governing homelands, and the "independent" homelands break up crowds, attempt to enforce the laws against demonstrations, take revenge, and generally try to "keep the lid on." Many of the police officers assigned to townships are black, as are all of the officers below the top ranks in the homelands. Most of the blacks who are killed in these instances are either protesters or innocent bystanders. The majority of all deaths in the unrest since September 1984 have been caused by the police force and the Defence Force. Few police officers are killed in these circumstances.

2. Killings of "collaborators" by the "comrades." These include the grisly "necklace" deaths, persons killed by having a gasoline-filled tire burned around their necks. The South African government claims that there were 172 necklace deaths between March 1 and June 5, 1986, plus 112 other deaths of "collaborators," 1,125 homes fire-bombed, 347 businesses damaged, and 11 churches damaged.[8] The necklace is a "trademark" kind of killing, and the government statistics may at least be a ballpark figure. Responsibility for

most property destruction is much more open to question, although the comrades are possibly to blame. Churches were much more likely to have been damaged by government-approved vigilantes.

3. Violence by black vigilantes. The vigilantes are supporters of the status quo who see not only the comrades but UDF and its affiliates as totally undesirable. There is ample documentation that the South African police have actively assisted vigilantes in some instances and stood by and watched their killing and destruction in others.* Since the Haysom report, vigilantes have committed their awesome destruction in Crossroads, with thousands made homeless and scores killed. The government then refused to let churches in white areas continue to offer refuge to those whose homes were destroyed or to allow the refugees to go back into Crossroads to rebuild the shacks which were their homes. Vigilante violence is government violence.

Comrades vs. Vigilantes

Who are the comrades? Who are the vigilantes?

The comrades are usually young men with an average age of about fifteen years. Their high visibility has caused the resistance to be called a youth movement. Although the name is used throughout the country, there is no indication of centralized planning, direction, or leadership among them. There is sometimes a core of organization within a township, particularly when the comrades move from punishment of collaborators to attempt to form the beginnings of alternative government within a township. Such alternatives include parks and people's courts. The goal which unifies comrades is punishment and intimidation of collaborators with apartheid. Black police officers, city council members,

---

*For an excellent report on black vigilantes, see *Apartheid's Private Army,* by Nicholas Haysom, published by the Catholic Institute of International Relations, London, 1986.

and township officials are the targets. In some townships, police have had to be moved into fenced compounds for their protection. Much of the activity of comrades seems ad hoc, with action developing on the scene as opportunity arises. Leadership is also diffused. The comrades have ignored the pleas of people like Bishop Tutu and Allan Boesak to stop using the necklace.

The vigilantes go by different group names in different places. The movement began in the homelands with the support of homeland leaders to protect those leaders and to help fulfill their goals. Vigilantes committed numerous atrocities in KwaNdebele, where nearby Africans resisted inclusion in the KwaNdebele territory. In Crossroads, one of the names given the vigilantes was "the fathers." This misleading, kindly name emphasized the desire to teach the young a lesson. There is an understandable tension between generations in the townships as parents look askance at youth striking out fearlessly against the government. However, that tension has not produced the vigilantes. Only in Crossroads did "fathers" go forth implementing a burnt-earth policy, displacing mainly women and small children, destroying houses and killing as the comrades tried unsuccessfully to defend their territory. Vigilantes accomplished in a few days what the government had been unable to accomplish in years—the massive removal of people from Crossroads.

Although there were black police officers, black members of the Army, and black informers in Zimbabwe and Mozambique during their struggle for independence, the development of the black vigilantes is a new element of terror and divisiveness in South Africa. David Beresford in a feature story calls the vigilantes "Botha's black warriors."[9]

White vs. White

Although they are not yet as deadly as the black vigilantes, reactionary Afrikaners have split the white front in South Africa. In May 1986, the Afrikaner Resistance Movement (Afrikaner Weerstandsbeweging, AWB) successfully stopped a speech by Pik Botha, the Foreign Minister. After AWB was denied a permit to hold a public meeting at the Voortrekker Monument they said they would go ahead with the meeting anyway, and the government backed down and allowed the meeting. Although AWB has been in existence for more than a decade, in the past it was considered a fringe group. There are a number of smaller vigilante groups which have acted as hit squads against black leaders. Since police cooperate with the black vigilantes, it was alleged that they cooperated with AWB in breaking up the National Party meeting where Pik Botha was to speak. When the crowd refused to disperse after having taken over the platform and the hall, the police used tear gas—the first such attack by whites on whites. This open, violent split in the white ranks in South Africa will probably become more serious as black resistance increases and the government seeks some accommodation.

Where to from Here?

The struggle in South Africa is a struggle for power. In its broadest terms it is an effort to maintain white domination as blacks try to gain power. But there are a number of minor actors on the stage willing to hold power over a limited geographic area—right-wing whites seeking a white homeland and black homeland leaders hoping to rule over their own territory. A number of groups are in contention. There are the two white groups, conservatives and liberals, who sometimes will oppose one another and sometimes work together. The conservatives seek to maintain white domination. The more liberal whites will probably not have a group identity but will cooperate with black-led organizations.

There are three black-led groups. One such group is non-racial, including ANC, UDF, and the Congress of South African Trade Unions. A second is the Black Consciousness group of PAC, AZAPO, the National Forum, and a few black trade unions. The third black-led group is that of Chief Gatsha Buthelezi and his followers (see Chapter 10). (A possible fourth group is a coalition of homeland leaders.) The South African policy of divide and rule—identify everyone within ethnic divisions—seems certain to bear more evil fruit before liberation finally comes about.

It appears in 1986 that the end for white domination is in sight, even though it may still be a few years away. There are three distinct changes in this period from past periods of crisis.

1. Blacks expect to end white oppression and control.

2. After Soweto, thousands of young blacks, mostly male, left South Africa. In the current period of resistance they are not leaving. They are staying to participate in the struggle at home and to witness the victory.

3. The "unrest" is not just in urban areas. Overt resistance has spread throughout the country.

It is clear that repression, resistance, and response will continue and grow, with a great deal of violence on all sides. The Commonwealth Group experience (see Chapter 6) has made it clear that South Africa is not yet ready for reasonable negotiations.

A word beginning to creep into conversations about South Africa is "Lebanon." Must South Africa pass through a stage of armed fiefdoms before reunion? It is possible.

More people are talking about external military intervention to create stability. Such stability might create an opportunity for reorganization and elections, much as temporary British oversight did in Zimbabwe in 1980. Conor Cruise O'Brien suggests the possibility of joint U.S. and U.S.S.R. action through the UN.[10] Speaking at a news conference in Washington on June 19, 1986, Jesse Jackson called for the United States to prepare for military intervention on behalf of the black majority. The Organization of African Unity and the frontline states have been mentioned as candidates for military intervention. The UN peacekeeping force did operate in the Congo (now Zaire). There is no authority for intervening in South Africa the way Britain did in Zimbabwe, and external military intervention does not seem likely short of total disaster, which is, of course, a possibility.

The powerful South African military forces may well take control in the face of the collapse of the civilian government. The military is already playing a major role in the civilian government. Will the military be more repressive or more open to negotiations?

The immediate road ahead for South Africa is dangerous and uncertain. South Africa and the world must hope for a South African leadership able to rise to the challenge of nation building. The potential is there. The world must be prepared to help those South Africans working for an inclusive state and for a society that is nonracial, democratic, just, and humane.

5

The Geopolitics of
South Africa

Countries are, of course, affected by events outside their borders as well as by those within. This is true even when, as in the case of South Africa, there are vigorous elements pressing for isolation from the rest of the world. From the outside, economic, sports, and arts boycotts are organized as campaigns against apartheid. South African representatives often find their participation challenged at international conferences. The United Nations approved a voluntary arms embargo against South Africa in 1963 after the Sharpeville Massacre and a mandatory arms embargo in November 1977 after the Soweto uprising. In 1981 a campaign for economic sanctions was renewed within the UN General Assembly. It has become a continuing campaign.

Forces from within the South African government also push toward isolation. Many white South Africans believe that apartheid is a domestic matter and that the system is either satisfactory, and should be of no concern to the rest of the world, or a problem which can best be solved if South Africa is left alone to deal with it.

These pressures toward isolation can't change the fact that South Africa is very much part of the world; it is a resource-rich country with highly developed industry and commerce intricately linked with the Western economy. The United States and other countries consider South Africa economically and strategically important. Further, as the last white-ruled country in Africa and the only country in the world where racial privilege is enforced by law, South Africa necessarily attracts international attention.

Regional Relationships

South Africa is connected by history, geography, and economic interests to the other nine states of southern Africa—Angola, Botswana, Lesotho, Malawi, Mozambique, Namibia, Swaziland, Zambia, Zimbabwe. The slave trade and the discovery of gold brought Europeans to the coast of Angola, and Arabs and Europeans to the coast of Mozambique. It was from the Cape of Good Hope in the seventeenth century that settlers from Europe began the push north and east into the interior of South Africa. Cecil Rhodes, from England, provided the initiative for opening the interior beyond South Africa in order to develop mines and extend the British Empire, and the majority of early settlers were British. As a result of Rhodes's efforts and the establishment of missionaries such as Livingstone, the center of southern Africa became a British colonial territory during the latter half of the nineteenth century. Later, Afrikaner farmers, who looked upon South Africa instead of Europe as the motherland, eventually became an economic and political power base within the areas now comprising Zambia and Zimbabwe, and to a lesser extent Botswana.

Communication flowed north and south as roads and railroads were built from the interior to South Africa and its ports. Other railroads were built to connect Zambia, Zimbabwe, and Malawi to ports in Mozambique, and another through Angola, with the result that southern Africa was further developed as an interdependent economic unit. The only northern commercial routes out of the area, other than by air, are an all-weather highway built with U.S. assistance and a railroad from Zambia to Dar es Salaam built by the People's Republic of China after Zambia's independence. The use of the railroad has been severely curtailed because of difficulties with Dar es Salaam's limited port capabilities.

Botswana (then Bechuanaland), Lesotho (then Basuto-land), and Swaziland were British protectorates. As South Africa's racial policies developed, British and South African

Major Railways of Southern Africa[1]

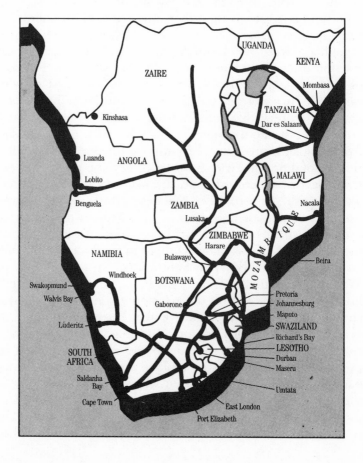

expectations that these countries would be joined to South Africa were dropped, and they became independent states in the late 1960s. They remain, however, closely connected to the South African economy and are part of the Southern Africa Customs Union, in which South Africa takes a leading role.

Malawi is the only African country currently maintaining full diplomatic relations with South Africa. South Africa has given economic assistance to Malawi, including a major grant to relocate the capital city. Men from Malawi work in South Africa's mines, although in much smaller numbers than in former years, and South Africa is Malawi's main trading partner.

Zambia is also tied economically to South Africa, buying food and some manufactured products and exporting some copper through South African ports. An alternative rail route for Zambia's exports through Angola remains unreliable because of guerrilla warfare waged against the Angolan government.

Zimbabwe has many ties with South Africa now, and had an even closer relationship in its former days as Southern Rhodesia. The relationship was intensified during the days of the Unilateral Declaration of Independence (UDI) as South Africa filled many of the economic gaps created by the UN boycott against the government of Ian Smith. Many whites now in Zimbabwe originally came from South Africa, and many of Zimbabwe's present black leaders received part of their education there. Whites travel extensively between the two countries for vacations and on business, and South African individuals and companies remain the largest outside investors in Zimbabwe.

Like Zimbabwe, Mozambique has been closely tied into the South African economy. Mozambican men working in the mines of South Africa continue to be an important source of foreign exchange for their country. In October 1986, in retaliation for sabotage attempts, presumed to be by guerrillas based in Mozambique, South Africa announced the end of recruitment of workers from Mozambique and the termination of all current contracts as they expire. This will be a serious blow to the Mozambique economy if the policy is actually implemented. Cabora Bassa, a large hydroelectric plant in the center of Mozambique, supplies electricity almost exclusively for South Africa. South African personnel, mostly white, operate ports in Mozambique and are vital to the operation of the railroad.

Angola has been the country of southern Africa least related to South Africa. Since 1975, the guerrilla fight to free Namibia from South African control has created a virtual state of war between South Africa and Angola. SWAPO, the main Namibian liberation movement, operates from bases in Angola, and South Africa stages both ground and air attacks in Angola in retaliation. Furthermore, South Africa supports UNITA (National Union for the Total Independence of Angola), composed of dissident Angolan forces, in its guerrilla warfare against the Angolan government, and this exacerbates tensions between the countries.

The mineral-rich and sparsely populated Namibia is closely tied to South Africa economically as well as politically. Most of the country's food and consumer goods are imported from South Africa. The two harbors, Lüderitz and Walvis Bay, are operated by South African Railways. Namibia is the second-largest producer of diamonds, after South Africa, and its entire output is exported by a subsidiary of De Beers, Consolidated Mines of South Africa, Ltd. The once rich but now dangerously depleted fishing grounds off the Namibian coast and the fish-processing plants there were once second only to mining in economic importance.

South Africa has allowed other countries to exploit the many mineral resources of Namibia. The Tsumeb mine in northern Namibia is one of the larger base-metal mines in the world. It is jointly controlled by an American company, AMAX, and the Newmont Mining Corporation, which is owned by Anglo American, a British–South African company. Namibia is believed to be the third-largest source of uranium in the world and has the world's largest uranium oxide pit. The Rossing uranium mine at Swakopmund near Walvis Bay is particularly controversial. First, it was opened in 1976 in violation of the 1970 UN Security Council Resolution 283, which called on all states to take a series of measures designed to end any trade or commercial dealings and investments by their nationals in Namibia. Second, the uranium could contribute to South Africa's development of nuclear weapons.

Namibia is tied not only to South Africa but to other countries in southern Africa and to the world because of its history as a Mandated Territory. It is closely linked to its neighbors, Angola and Zambia, which have provided shelter to refugees and support to SWAPO and as a result have suffered attacks by the South African Defence Force. Lusaka, Zambia, is the home of the UN Institute for Namibia, where future administrators and leaders of Namibia are trained. Botswana has also accepted Namibian refugees.

South African Military Aggression

The international arms embargo notwithstanding, South Africa has developed a vigorous domestic arms industry which is heavily dependent on imports of foreign high-tech components. With sub rosa help from the West, Pretoria has developed a formidable military machine, enabling it to mount major operations against its neighbors with near-impunity.

In addition to military aggression into Angola, South Africa also has committed military aggression against Mozambique, Lesotho, Botswana, Zimbabwe, and Zambia. Although South Africa proclaims that its aggression is defensive to prevent ANC infiltration of guerrillas and weapons, there is clearly a large element of intentional destabilization in these attacks. South Africa wants neighbors to be client states and does not want to confront the ideological impact of successful nonracial states in southern Africa.

The destabilization effort is most evident in Mozambique. The Mozambique National Resistance Movement (MNR) is a guerrilla movement of Portuguese and dissident Mozambicans who have not accepted the FRELIMO government of Mozambique. The MNR was given primary support by Ian Smith during his days of leadership in Southern Rhodesia. South Africa became the patron after the fall of the Smith government.

Under considerable duress from the multiple difficulties of Mozambique, President Samora Machel of Mozambique and then Prime Minister (now State President) Botha signed the Nkomati accord on May 16, 1984. This accord was meant to stop infiltration of ANC into South Africa from Mozambique and the infiltration from South Africa of personnel and supplies for MNR in Mozambique, even though South Africa still had not admitted giving assistance to MNR. Mozambique kept the agreement, and a number of ANC personnel left the country. South Africa, however, continued to support MNR, a fact confirmed by the seizure of documents at an MNR base in Sofala Province in August 1983. President Botha eventually admitted the violation. The growing strength of MNR makes continued support from South Africa seem to be a certainty. In spite of Mozambican efforts to comply with the Nkomati agreement, Mozambique was again subjected to a military raid by South Africa at the same time as Zimbabwe, Zambia, and Botswana in May 1986.

President Samora Machel of Mozambique was killed in a plane crash in South Africa near the Mozambique border on October 19, 1986. The change in leadership is not expected to change the uneasy relationship between Mozambique and South Africa.

Destabilization in Zimbabwe

South African attempts at destabilization in Zimbabwe have been both overt and covert. Soon after Zimbabwe's independence, South Africa recalled railroad locomotives that were on loan to Zimbabwe. The loss of the locomotives would have paralyzed Zimbabwe's transportation system. International pressure got the recall reversed. South Africa also sent all Zimbabwe workers home, a threat South Africa holds over neighboring countries, all of which, like South Africa itself, have high levels of unemployment. The South African-supported MNR sabotaged the oil pipeline to Zimbabwe and a railroad between Zimbabwe and Mozambique so frequently that Zimbabwe soldiers must patrol both of those extensive areas in Mozambique. In August 1982, South African military personnel, mission unknown, were captured in Zimbabwe. The Zimbabwe government charges South Africa with the training and supply of Zimbabwe dissidents. The evidence has not been found, but the history of South African aggression against its neighbors lends credibility to the accusation.

The supplying of MNR after the Nkomati agreement and the military raid in Harare in Zimbabwe in May 1986 seem to indicate that the South African military may be acting independently of the civilian government in "security" matters. Just before the raid in Harare the *South African Digest,* on May 2, 1986, reprinted an article from *The Star* stating that "Prime Minister Robert Mugabe had thus far honored his undertaking not to allow Zimbabwe to be used as a staging ground for armed activities against South Africa."

It may be that the South African military operates independently, or perhaps State President Botha automatically approves any proposed military action, irrespective of other commitments. In an interview with *Beeld,* a Johannesburg newspaper, Botha said: "My years as Minister of Defence were among the happiest in the past 50 years. The growth of the Defence Force and the development of South Africa's armaments industry and the particular comradeship which I experienced in that organization were sources of great joy to me."[2]

South African military and economic threats and action

have successfully pressured Botswana, Swaziland, Mozambique, Lesotho, and Zimbabwe into agreements to prevent infiltration of ANC guerrillas and to deny them facilities for training. South African economic pressure was a major cause of the fall of the former government of Lesotho.

The overt military actions of South Africa in neighboring countries have resulted in condemnation even by the United States and the United Kingdom, but little else.

The SADCC Response

No matter how much they detest apartheid, and in spite of the military aggression against them, the other states of southern Africa have found it impossible to sever every relationship with South Africa because of the historical alignment of trade and transportation. The eight majority-rule countries of southern Africa, together with Tanzania, have established an organization (Southern African Development Coordination Conference, SADCC) and a process, including periodic conferences, to seek ways to improve agricultural production, communications, and trade, thus increasing their collective self-sufficiency and decreasing their dependence on South Africa. The SADCC agreement was signed in Lusaka on April 1, 1980. A small secretariat for SADCC works out of Botswana. Each country has taken one field for which it will develop expertise and provide leadership to the others. A number of Western countries have made grants for SADCC-sponsored projects. The practical change in lessening dependence on South Africa is small, but the continuing communication and cooperation among these countries bodes well for the long term.

The economic dependence of the states of the region is an important element in South Africa's prosperity. This dependence also lessens South Africa's isolation from the rest of the world. The South African government has proposed to use these interrelationships as a basis for a "constellation" of southern African states, including the "independent" homelands. For obvious political reasons, no common market approach to southern Africa is possible as long as minority rule continues in South Africa. An economically strong southern Africa confederation may develop after majority rule is achieved.

The Independence Movement

From the 1950s to the 1970s, majority rule in Africa progressed from the northern countries southward. White South Africans considered themselves insulated by the Portuguese colonies of Mozambique and Angola, by white-dominated Southern Rhodesia, by an economically dependent Botswana and a politically controlled Namibia. When Mozambique and Angola gained freedom from Portugal in 1975, and Zimbabwe gained majority rule in 1980, the situation was radically altered. Still, a political transformation in South Africa seems remote.

Why have the forces which moved the other African states to majority rule not yet moved South Africa? The African countries that gained majority governments in this period had different histories of colonization from that of South Africa. From the formation of the Union of South Africa in 1910, white minority rule in South Africa has not been a traditional colonialism. Most white South Africans do not feel linked to a European homeland to which they may return, nor does any European or other national group have even nominal political authority in South Africa. In all the other situations, there was an external power to grant independence, however reluctantly and belatedly. In South Africa majority rule can be gained only from within.

Although there were some whites in both Zimbabwe and Mozambique who saw "one person, one vote" as a threat to their jobs, the fear of black competition on the labor market is far greater and more real in South Africa than it was in any other African country. (See Chapter 7 for a report on African labor unions.)

Nonetheless, the same forces which brought increasingly irresistible pressure against colonialism in Africa continue to build up against white rule in South Africa. There are forces such as those created by Pan Africanism, the Organization of African Unity, the independence and increasing power of Third World countries around the world, and the development of a Third World majority in the UN's "one nation, one vote" General Assembly.

Colonialism was interwoven with racism, the major problem in South Africa. Efforts to deal with racism elsewhere, notably in the United States, have had an impact on South Africa. Black consciousness in the United States and in South Africa have undergone parallel and independent developments, but the movement in the 1960s in the United States had a definite impact on the South African movement. Conversely, the leaders of independent African countries have inspired black civil rights leaders in the United States.

Black and white South Africans hold different views on the results of the elimination of colonialism from the continent and the heightened world awareness of racism. Both recognize an impact on their own country. Blacks see that most of the governments of their neighboring states grant dignity to all their citizens, black and white, seek to equalize economic opportunity as well as political status, and work to overcome both the spirit and the effects of racism. Blacks also see majority governments as supportive of their own struggle for liberation.

Most white South Africans feared the momentum of change as the movement for independence pressed south. They believe that African rule is corrupt, destructive of national economies, and subject to coups. They believe there are few free elections. Many cite Idi Amin of Uganda as a typical African leader. This image is what they expect for South Africa under a "one person, one vote" structure (and, they usually add, one election). Their view of independent Africa is maintained and reinforced by a pattern of limited access to information about events in other parts of Africa and by the government's official version of events.

Some white South Africans, however, also admit the inevitability of majority rule and seek ways to accommodate themselves to this change. A major Afrikaans newspaper, reporting on the election of Mugabe in Zimbabwe, exhorted white South Africa to acknowledge its relevance to their own country, saying: "We must learn that to try to preserve everything is to lose everything."

Anti-Communism

Anti-Communism fuels much of white South Africa's fear of and resistance to change. An anti-Communist hysteria is orchestrated and promoted by some leaders in order to strengthen commitment to the present system. In this view, Communists get all the credit or all the blame for the resistance to apartheid. Paradoxically, white anti-Communism prompts more black interest in Communism than action by Communists themselves. An illegal Communist Party does exist underground in South Africa, and a few members have been prosecuted.

Much of South Africa's concern centers on Communist support for liberation movements. The Soviet Union supports the African National Congress (ANC). The Pan Africanist Congress (PAC) has received support from China.

South African leaders are far more concerned about the Soviet Union than about China. The Chinese have maintained a low profile in Africa, giving some economic assistance and military training to Tanzania, in addition to some aid to liberation groups. The largest aid project supported by the Chinese is the railroad that links Zambia to the Tanzanian port of Dar es Salaam, a project turned down by the World Bank and Western governments, including the United States, as not economically feasible.

SWAPO receives strong support from Moscow, and South Africa continually raises that issue. Preoccupation with

Communism obscures the reality that liberation movements are, first of all, nationalist. They are also pragmatic and will accept help from wherever it comes. Communist countries have helped most of the liberation movements of southern Africa, which have often sought support from Western nations and been turned down. In spite of these relationships, the new nations, once free, act in their own perceived interests. Both the United States and the Soviet Union have often been disappointed with the consistent nonalignment of independent southern African states. The liberation movements have never been willing to trade one colonial overlord for another.

Zimbabwe is an excellent example of this. Robert Mugabe, now Prime Minister, was seen by most whites in South Africa and Southern Rhodesia as the epitome of Communist evil when he led his guerrilla forces against Rhodesia. These whites expected him, if he won power, to establish a Communist government which would be ruthless in dealing with white leaders and in suppressing civil rights and economic free enterprise. It was expected that representatives of Communist governments would be welcomed with open arms. However, the first embassy established in Zimbabwe was that of the United States—on the first day of independence. There were many months of negotiations before the embassy of the Soviet Union was accepted. Seven years after independence, Zimbabwe still has a mixed economy.

The United States is also obsessively concerned with Communism. Therefore, both South Africa and the United States have focused on the presence of troops in Africa from Communist countries, while ignoring those from other parts of the world, such as France. Black Africans express concern about the role of foreign troops from whatever country. They ask: To whom are the troops responsible? At whose invitation are they present? Whose interests do they protect?

Not only is anti-Communism used by South Africa to solidify internal resistance to change; it is also exploited to gain support for the current South African regime from the

United States and other Western nations. South Africa's minerals and the sea route around the Cape are seen by some as of strategic interest to the "free world." The Reagan administration seems to have bought this argument. Significant numbers of white South Africans believe, or hope, that if a violent showdown comes, the United States can be relied on for support to "defeat Communism." Western support for apartheid is justified by the East–West conflict.

Fear of Communist attack from outside or within gives justification for a military machine that is stronger than those of any combination of the surrounding states. There is rigidly enforced military conscription for every able-bodied white male. White males remain liable for compulsory military duty to age sixty-five. Other races are in the armed forces as volunteers. All races may now receive training in the use of arms and white women are actively recruited into the military. Emergency legislation and planning provide for the total mobilization of people and industry, including U.S.-owned industry. The armed forces are used regularly as part of the internal security operation in cases of civilian demonstrations and disturbances.

There is a probability that South Africa has produced a nuclear weapon. It has the capability to do so, which adds a new dimension to South Africa's destructive potential. Nuclear weapons, useless for civil wars, pose a threat to countries such as Nigeria, which has been a leader against apartheid. Nuclear weapons in the hands of South Africa, which refuses to sign the UN nonproliferation treaty, represent one more dangerous development in nuclear proliferation.

Soviet Policy

Because of the fear of Soviet Communism expressed by South Africa, it is important to assess Soviet policies in the area, even though these are difficult to know with certainty. As with most countries, Soviet foreign policy is a mix of ideological and pragmatic elements. Ideologically, the Soviets appear to operate on two bases. First, there is a commitment to socialism and, when possible, to its extension to other societies, which leads to the support of liberation movements in a number of places. Second, the superpower conflict gives rise to anti-Americanism, an ideological stance whose mirror image is U.S. anti-Sovietism. Pragmatically, the Soviet Union seeks to support its perceived national interest around the world, befriending potential allies, especially in economically or militarily strategic locations, and trying to limit and undermine U.S. influence.

One way to understand Soviet policies in southern Africa is to look at the record of Soviet involvements elsewhere in Africa. These policies have seldom been successful in establishing lasting influence. Starting with Ghana in 1966, the Soviet Union has been invited out of as many countries as those with which it has been able to establish long-term relationships. At one time, Egypt, Sudan, and Somalia were three of the largest recipients of Soviet military aid to Africa, but Soviet forces were subsequently expelled from all three (Sudan in 1972, Egypt in 1975, and Somalia in 1978). Soviet involvement in Guinea ended in 1979. In recent years, the U.S.S.R. has concentrated its attentions in Africa on four countries—Algeria, Libya, Ethiopia, and Angola. Involvement in the first three of these has much to do with the superpower conflict of interests in the Middle East and the Persian Gulf area.

In Angola, heavy Soviet and Cuban involvement began after October 1975 when South African and Zairean troops invaded to try to prevent the Soviet-supported MPLA (Popular Movement for the Liberation of Angola) from gaining control of the newly independent country. In no case has the Soviet Union committed large numbers of its own troops to African countries. In many instances, the Soviet Union and the People's Republic of China have supported opposing liberation groups, an extension of their own ideological and strategic conflict. This was true in Southern Rhodesia and remains so in Angola. Soviet involvement in Africa seems to take into account its competition with China as well as with the United States.

While it is obvious that the Soviet Union and its allies are involved in the African continent, it is also clear that this involvement has changed in response to changing conditions within the African countries. The Soviet Union has not been able to "call the shots" or achieve the stable relationships it may have wished for. In no case has the Soviet Union tried to cut off the access of the West to the continent's mineral resources or to seize Western economic interests. U.S. firms continue to operate in both Algeria and Angola, for example. These states, despite reliance on the Soviet Union, invite and encourage U.S. business interests and investments. In fact, trade between the Soviet Union and South Africa, though small, has been increasing and frequent reports tell of Soviet and South African collaboration to stabilize the prices of gold, diamonds, and platinum on the world market.

There is little evidence that the Soviet Union is trying to establish itself strongly throughout Africa. This may be partly the result of its unwillingness or inability to supply the economic assistance required to sustain such a campaign. In any event, Soviet experience and overextension in Afghanistan would seem likely to cool ambitions for political and military expansion to control any African countries. The U.S.S.R. is aware of the attitudes of the African nations themselves, which welcome no overlord even as they accept economic and military aid from whatever source. Soviet policy in Africa seems unlikely to change in the foreseeable future. There is little reason to expect that the Soviet Union will attempt any major alterations in its relations with the countries of Africa.

Insofar as South Africa is concerned, any threat to the present regime arises from internal dissent rather than from armed invasion by the U.S.S.R. or its allies. For South Africa, as has been true for so many other times and places, external "threat" is a handy justification for tightening internal control.

North–South Division

In addition to the East–West division, the North–South world division also affects South Africa. The latter division arises not from political systems but from differences in levels of development. The richer nations are concentrated in the Northern Hemisphere and the poorer nations in the Southern Hemipshere. In the United Nations, there are increasing demands and pressures from the nonaligned nations for the North to accept greater responsibility for its role in the poverty of the South. White South Africa identifies, in many ways, with the North. Its cultural heritage, level of personal income, and increasingly industrialized economic base are most consistent with the North; but what is not consistent is its minority racial status.

Thus in terms of affluence, white South Africa identifies with the North, and in terms of economic and political structures with the West. Black South Africa shares neither identification. Its ties are clearly to its own continent and, therefore, to the South. Many black South Africans and the liberation movements reject the economic inequality and domination which they see as part of the South African version of state-managed capitalism. They, as well as a growing group of nonaligned nations, reject the Soviet-model socialism as their model. They seek an alternative form of socialism which grows out of their own experience and which will bring about democracy with a more equitable distribution of resources. To make the point that they seek these new ways, the countries of eastern and southern Africa often describe their political and economic systems and goals as African socialism.

U.S. Policy

After decades of neglect, the United States began to pay serious attention to the continent of Africa following World War II. Uncertainty about the relative importance to the United States of various regions of the continent (northern, Arab; tropical, black African; southern, predominantly colonial and white-dominated in 1945) has persisted to this day. Colonialism has almost disappeared. The African caucus, with other Third World support, carries considerable influence at the United Nations. Great mineral wealth has been exploited in southern Africa, largely by white regimes, and oil has been found in North and West Africa. Thus, the continent has changed greatly since 1945.

For decades changing administrations in Washington have followed a relatively consistent policy: keep on good terms with all African nations, but cater especially to those whose raw materials, markets, investment opportunities, and strategic location are the most important to the U.S. national interest. U.S. officials were disconcerted when they found that a neutral or balanced posture among competing interests has been almost impossible.

Black nations, newly liberated from European colonialism, could not ignore the remaining minority regimes or their racial policies. They sought sympathy and support from the United States, a major power whose history and rhetoric suggested understanding of their needs. On many occasions, however, they felt rebuffed as they saw the United States lean toward European allies in NATO or toward conservative white minority regimes, presumably for strategic reasons. South Africa emphasized affinities with the United States and encouraged a growing economic relationship, with considerable success.

U.S. African policy over several administrations has been fashioned to satisfy various disparate interests on the home front and to support a foreign policy designed to check the

Soviet Union. Access to vital minerals and protection of the sea route around the Cape were given priority. Only in the 1980s has the growing importance of trade with black Africa (for example, oil from Nigeria and chrome from Zimbabwe), coupled with some increasing sensitivity to human rights issues abroad influenced by U.S. civil rights efforts, caused the United States to take the question of South Africa seriously. Increased public opposition to apartheid has also sensitized U.S. government awareness.

U.S. administrations have had shared goals in their policies toward South Africa, although priorities have differed. These goals include countering Soviet influence, promoting individual human rights, and maintaining access to strategic minerals. Secondary goals involve making some accommodation among conflicting interests of the U.S. public as well as the conflicting interests of the international community.

"Constructive engagement" is still a policy that engages the attention and the interests of only a small privileged stratum of South Africans. It relies almost entirely on white-led change, as designed and defined by a regime that is becoming more embattled by the day. And it ignores the needs, the politics and passions of the black majority in South Africa. The policy will continue to fail.

—Sanford Ungar and Peter Vale, "South Africa: Why Constructive Engagement Failed"[3]

The Reagan administration gave its South African policy a beautiful euphemism, "constructive engagement." The Carter administration might have called its policy "constructive confrontation." Neither administration can document much beneficial change in South Africa as a result of its efforts, but the two distinct policies clearly attract different groups of people in the United States, in South Africa, and in the rest of the international community. Most white South Africans, for example, are strongly anti-Carter and pro-Reagan. Those in power in South Africa are concerned about official U.S. actions and views.

Constructive engagement has included disavowing the Carter policy, usually accepting the South African government's evaluation as to what constitutes "reform," relaxing export controls, a vigorous campaign against sanctions and boycotts (including a number of UN vetoes), approval of delay of Namibian independence pending removal of Cuban troops from Angola, not "taking sides" between whites and blacks, increased military consultation and economic cooperation, less condemnation of apartheid, and, in general, a much friendlier tilt toward the South African government.

Public pressure in the United States has "bent" constructive engagement beyond the designers' wishes. To avoid stricter sanctions being enacted by Congress, President Reagan inaugurated minor sanctions in 1985.* Because of its symbolic importance in South Africa, probably the most significant was the banning of the importation of gold Krugerrands. Reagan omitted the congressional attempt to ban new investment.

Constructive engagement suffered an important defeat near the end of the 1986 congressional session when broad sanctions against South Africa became law with an overwhelming override of President Reagan's veto of the legislation. The new law bans most new U.S. investment in South Africa, ends landing rights in the U.S. for South African Airways, and prohibits imports of South African coal, iron, steel, uranium, textiles, and agricultural products. Other temporary sanctions created by executive order become permanent. The law provides for termination or modification of the sanctions in case of specific changes in South Africa.

---

* See *Backgrounder: The Reagan South Africa Computer Ban: An Analysis of New Export Regulations from the Commerce Dept.*, AFSC/NARMIC, Nov. 1985.

It is estimated that the sanctions will cost South Africa about $700 million annually in exports.

> Well, when the Polish Government applied martial law in Poland, who applied sanctions, and unilaterally at that? Why, it was the self-same US that can't see its way to doing half of what it did against the Polish Government and the Russians. The US Government does not really care about Blacks. Poles are different. They are White.
>
> —Bishop Desmond Tutu[4]

Under the Reagan administration, the Clark Amendment, which prohibited assistance to anti-government forces in Angola, was repealed. U.S. aid is again being given to UNITA (National Union for the Total Independence of Angola), led by Jonas Savimbi. UNITA, a legitimate liberation movement during the struggle for independence from Portugal, has continued extensive guerrilla warfare against the government of independent Angola. UNITA is supported both economically and militarily by South Africa. South African policy and U.S. policy join in being pro-UNITA because the Angolan government is Marxist and assumed to be a client state of the U.S.S.R.

Chester Crocker, Assistant Secretary of State for Africa and architect of the Reagan South African policy, as well as a spokesperson for the Carter administration, made much of the U.S. lack of power to change South African policy. On the other hand, there is much African opinion that the United States has such tremendous power that, if there were any will for it, the United States could turn things around in South Africa. There is some truth in each view.

The authority of the United States is nil, and its power is severely limited in ability to cause internal change in a strong, independent country such as South Africa. However, the limitations of power do not excuse limiting efforts for change or failure to clarify the U.S. abhorrence of apartheid. Chapter 9 suggests types of action the U.S. government might take.

The administration has voiced public disapproval of South African military aggression against its neighbors, and on one occasion recalled the U.S. ambassador for a few months and recalled the U.S. military attaché in May 1986. The United States objected to South Africa's efforts toward an internal settlement in Namibia which bypasses the UN plan. However, independence for Namibia, a top-priority southern African objective for the Reagan administration back in 1981, seems as far away now as then.

The Soviet and South African governments were delighted by the American use of the veto in the UN Security Council (August 31, 1981) against a formal condemnation of the South African armed forces' incursion into Angola. Although the motion was not well-worded, this veto has infuriated many of the three-quarters of the people of the world who are humiliated by white South Africa's racial policies. It has strengthened Mr. Pieter Botha and his South African cabinet in the belief that they can count on American protection. It has obliged the friends and allies of the U.S. to stand apart from it. These are heavy prices to pay. They include some practical prices in the Third World. An internationally acceptable settlement in Namibia—one that might have got the Cubans out of Angola—will now be harder to get. Next time America needs the help of a third party, as it needed Algeria's to get its hostages out of Iran, some of the necessary thrust may be found no longer to exist. Support at the UN for resolutions condemning Russia—as, for instance, after the invasion of Afghanistan—may not be so forthcoming

in the future. America has forfeited, at least for a
time, some influence in guiding economic development in black Africa and in moderating its
extremists. By spitting into the wind of change it
has encouraged the Qaddafis of the continent.

—*The Economist*,[5]

However South African policy is articulated and implemented, it is clear that an informed, vocal American public
opinion has had some impact and continues to be important
for keeping the United States from supporting oppressive
regimes such as South Africa's, especially when it appears
that the support arises from ill-conceived strategic and economic concerns that discount the human factor.

6

International Pressure on Apartheid

South Africa faces increasing criticism abroad. Many international organizations such as sporting groups, labor organizations, and religious bodies have been critical of apartheid. They have passed resolutions, banned South African representatives from attendance at meetings, contributed to the support of liberation groups, helped refugees from South Africa and Namibia, boycotted South African products, divested themselves of stock in corporations doing business in South Africa, and found many other ways to express their displeasure. The Organization of African Unity and the United Nations have maintained continuous protest against South African policies. Even international corporations have become a force outside South Africa involved in the political issues of apartheid. It is important to examine international pressures on apartheid and to try to assess the effectiveness of that pressure.

The Organization of African Unity

In 1963, at Addis Ababa, the Organization of African Unity was formed. The OAU is a voluntary association of African states which seeks to address continental issues. While the countries are economically and politically diverse, they have always been in agreement in their opposition to apartheid. The OAU has spearheaded international action related to South Africa's minority government. At the time of its inception, many African states were still colonies, and six of its original fifteen resolutions affirmed the OAU's support for liberation movements in the Portuguese colonies, Southern Rhodesia, Namibia, and South Africa. Resolution 12 of the charter document established a "Special Fund to be raised by voluntary contribution of Member States . . . to supply the necessary practical and financial aid to the various African national liberation movements."

The OAU adopted a nine-point policy specifically aimed at South Africa to "put an end to the South African Government's criminal policy of apartheid and wipe out racial discrimination in all its forms." The points centered on sanctions, diplomatic isolation, support for efforts within the United Nations, and appeals to all governments to support the struggle against the South African regime. The final point expressed "appreciation for the efforts of the Federal Government of the United States of America to put an end to these intolerable malpractices which are likely seriously to deteriorate relations between the African peoples and governments on the one hand and the people and government of the United States on the other." In the 1960s there was hope and expectation that the United States would use its moral and economic power to help bring majority rule in South Africa.

In 1969, at a meeting in Lusaka, Zambia, fourteen states from eastern and central Africa agreed upon a manifesto which said:

> We have always preferred and we will prefer to achieve liberation without physical violence. We would prefer to negotiate rather than to destroy, to talk rather than kill. We do not advocate violence; we advocate an end to violence against

human dignity which is now being perpetrated by the oppressors of Africa. If peaceful progress to emancipation were
possible, or if changed circumstances were to make it possible in the future, we would urge our brothers in the resistance movements to use peaceful methods of struggle *even at
the cost of some compromise on the timing of change* [emphasis
added].

This manifesto was subsequently adopted in September 1969
by the Organization of African Unity and, later, by the
General Assembly of the United Nations.

In spite of their reluctance to use force, liberation movements in Africa have all relied on armed force, as well as
negotiations, to undermine the status quo and to stimulate
international pressure to support them. In 1972, at its meeting at Rabat, Morocco, the OAU noted "with satisfaction
the progress made by the various Liberation Movements actively engaged in the armed struggle, particularly in Guinea-
Bissau, Mozambique, Angola and Namibia, which constitute a major development of far-reaching military, political
and social impact on the evolution of the armed liberation
struggle."[1]

The United Nations

From its earliest days the United Nations has dealt with
issues of human rights in South Africa. At the second session of the UN General Assembly in December 1946, a
complaint regarding the denial of human rights to Indian
people in South Africa was delivered by Mrs. Pandit of India. As other African nations gained freedom and membership in the UN, and as South Africa repeatedly defied UN
jurisdiction over Namibia, a series of resolutions condemning the racism of South Africa and its illegal rule in Namibia
were passed by the UN. In 1962 the General Assembly urged
that the members of the UN break diplomatic relations with
South Africa and that they cease to offer access to their fa-

cilities for its planes and ships. In 1963 a Security Council ban (Resolution 181) on sales of arms to South Africa was passed with United States and British support. It was made mandatory in 1977. A series of further resolutions and debates has followed. In 1979 alone, eighteen resolutions were passed against South African apartheid unanimously or by overwhelming majorities in the UN General Assembly. The General Assembly proclaimed 1982 as the International Year of Mobilization for Sanctions against South Africa. The "mobilization" did not bring much in the way of results. In December 1983 the General Assembly voted 124 to 16, with 10 abstentions, for mandatory sanctions, including an oil embargo. With the exception of the earlier arms embargo, mandatory sanctions were always vetoed in the Security Council by the United States, the United Kingdom, and sometimes France. In December 1984 the Security Council unanimously adopted a resolution calling on all countries to cease *buying* arms from South Africa. The resolution called for voluntary, not mandatory, action.

In addition to the series of resolutions passed by the General Assembly and the Security Council concerning apartheid within South Africa, the UN has focused a great deal of attention on South Africa's administration of Namibia. (The historical development of the Namibia problem and early UN action on it are reported in Chapter 2.)

In 1973 the General Assembly recognized SWAPO as the authentic representative of the Namibian people. On January 30, 1976, the Security Council adopted Resolution 385, again condemning the illegal control of Namibia by South Africa and calling for "free elections under the supervision and control of the United Nations . . . for the whole of Namibia as one political entity." By 1978 five Western nations—Canada, France, the Federal Republic of Germany, the United Kingdom, and the United States—brought to the Security Council a report of meetings they had held jointly in South Africa. Resolution 431 was then passed, calling for the appointment of a Special Representative who would ensure that conditions were established for free and fair elections in Namibia, the release of all Namibian political prisoners and the return of all refugees and others outside the territory, and a comprehensive cessation of all hostilities, with the South African and SWAPO armed forces restricted to their bases.

By September 1978, Resolution 435 established a United Nations Transition Assistance Group for a period of up to twelve months to ensure free elections in Namibia under UN supervision. SWAPO agreed to cooperate fully with these election plans. South Africa agreed in principle, but by October it was clear that South Africa was not prepared to implement Resolution 435. Instead, the South African government proceeded unilaterally, holding elections in Namibia in December, an act condemned subsequently and declared invalid and illegal by the UN General Assembly and the Security Council. This "internal settlement" arranged by South Africa resulted in the Democratic Turnhalle Alliance (DTA) government. The DTA was an alliance of many small, often ethnically based political parties. That government gave effective control to whites and black minority groups dependent on whites.

In January 1981, the UN sponsored a conference in Geneva between SWAPO and the South African government to try to negotiate the implementation of Resolution 435. A number of Namibian political parties were represented within the South African delegation. SWAPO again agreed to a cease-fire and an election at any time that would be acceptable to South Africa. The South African delegation was made up largely of DTA members. That delegation refused to take any steps toward implementation of the previous agreement on Resolution 435, asserting that UN supervision was unacceptable because the UN was prejudiced in favor of SWAPO. The conference broke up with nothing accomplished.

Because of South Africa's unwillingness to implement Resolution 435, another attempt was made in April 1981 to have the Security Council impose total sanctions against South Africa. The United States, France, and the United Kingdom joined in the veto of that resolution.

Meanwhile the fortunes of the DTA were going into a decline in Namibia, either in spite of or because of South African backing. Movement toward independence and a nonracial society was too slow for blacks and too fast for many whites. In September 1983 a number of Namibian groups, including most of those represented in the DTA, got together to form the Multi-Party Conference (MPC) as a replacement for the DTA in an effort to move Namibia toward "self-determination." The South African government was discussing a new constitution for Namibia, presumably another move toward an internal settlement. Once again the UN and many countries, including the United States, protested any settlement other than one under UN Resolution 435.

Another UN attempt at condemnation of South Africa by the Security Council followed South Africa's extensive military incursions into Angola in August 1981. There was a great deal of property damage and, according to South Africa, a thousand deaths. Although the invasion was justified by South Africa as an attempt to break up SWAPO guerrilla warfare, most of the dead were Angolans. The United States cast a lone veto against condemnation.

Although UN resolutions get the most press coverage and do not seem to result in much action, the UN is involved more quietly in many forms of assistance to Namibians and South Africans. A UN institute in Lusaka is training Namibians for the future administration of their country. Aid is given to political refugees and to refugees in camps from the war zones of Namibia and Angola. Many scholarships are given for attending universities. Material assistance is given to liberation movements. Travel documents are provided for those citizens of Namibia and South Africa who cannot get passports from their own country. An international platform is provided for those who might otherwise not be heard.

The Commonwealth

> Our work in South Africa has been a moving personal experience for every one of us. We arrived in the country when there was carnage in Alexandra. On the day of our final departure from Cape Town, Crossroads was on fire and a pall of smoke hung in the sky. We saw a country in upheaval and witnessed great human suffering. Even as we write, the killings continue.
> —*Mission to South Africa:*
> *The Commonwealth Report*[2]

The Commonwealth consists of Britain and forty-eight of its former colonies in a loose association. It played a key role in arranging the Lancaster House talks in London which brought the civil war in Southern Rhodesia to an end and started the process for elections to create an independent Zimbabwe. It has been increasingly active in trying to arrange a settlement in South Africa, although South Africa is no longer a member of the Commonwealth (see Chapter 2).

The Commonwealth meeting in Nassau in October 1985 appointed the seven-member "Commonwealth Group of Eminent Persons" to attempt a negotiating process to end apartheid and establish a "nonracial representative government" in South Africa.

The entire group made two trips to South Africa, where it was allowed free access to the African townships, visited Nelson Mandela, and had long conversations with P. W. Botha and other government leaders. The project was aborted in May 1986 when South Africa made military incursions into Zambia, Zimbabwe, and Botswana while the Commonwealth Group was in South Africa. The three countries attacked are members of the Commonwealth.

The basic proposal was for negotiations with black-selected

leaders of the black people, including ANC. The Group concluded: ". . . while the Government claims to be ready to negotiate, it is in truth not yet prepared to negotiate fundamental change, nor to countenance the creation of genuine democratic structures, nor to face the prospect of the end of white domination and white power in the foreseeable future. Its programme of reform does not end apartheid, but seeks to give it a less inhuman face. Its quest is power-sharing, but without surrendering overall white control."[3]

Subsequently, however, the South African government reported it still had the Commonwealth proposals under consideration.[4]

The report also noted: "After 18 months of persistent unrest, upheaval, and killings unprecedented in the country's history, the Government believes that it can contain the situation indefinitely by use of force. We were repeatedly told by Ministers that the government had deployed only a fraction of the power at its disposal. Although the Government's confidence may be valid in the short term, but at a great human cost, it is plainly misplaced in the longer term. South Africa is predominantly a country of black people. To believe that they can be indefinitely suppressed is an act of self-delusion."[5]

Following the failure of the Commonwealth Group to get negotiations going in South Africa, Prime Minister Thatcher of Britain met in London with the heads of state of six Commonwealth countries.* Mrs. Thatcher agreed to bans on new investment and on the promotion of tourism. The other leaders approved for their countries, and for recommendation to other Commonwealth members, a ban on air links, a ban on all agricultural products, a ban on all government procurement in South Africa, a ban on all new bank loans to either the public or the private sector, and a ban on the importation of coal, iron, and steel. Mrs. Thatcher also agreed to join the European Economic Community (EEC) in a ban on the importation of coal, iron, and steel from

---

* Australia, Bahamas, Canada, India, Zambia, and Zimbabwe.

South Africa, if the EEC agreed on that action. Subsequently, the EEC agreed to a ban on the importation of iron and steel, but not coal.

The Commonwealth will continue to be active on the South African issue.

Religious Organizations

In 1954, the World Council of Churches (WCC), without dissent but with a few abstentions, declared segregation based on race, color, or ethnic origin to be contrary to the Gospel and incompatible with Christian doctrine and the nature of the church of Christ. National church bodies around the world accepted the WCC statement against racism. But there has been a large gap between the acceptance of the statement at the national church level and acceptance by members in local churches. In the United States, leadership on racial policy in the national denominations was supported by black caucuses of the members, but national church policy has not always been translated into local unity or agreement.

The WCC's efforts for racial justice in South Africa during the 1950s and much of the 1960s were limited to encouraging and assisting South African churches to consult with one another. At that time all the major denominations in South Africa except the Roman Catholics were members of the WCC. The WCC initiated a worldwide study program on Christian responsibility in geographic areas of rapid social change. One such conference was held in South Africa in December 1959 with two hundred delegates, only nine of whom came from overseas.

After the Sharpeville Massacre on March 21, 1960, the South African churches, including the three branches of the white Dutch Reformed Church (DRC), requested the WCC to initiate a consultation on Christian responsibility in race relations. The result was the Cottesloe Consultation, where a number of papers prepared in advance by South African churches were discussed. The consultation agreed upon a statement in which many of the participants from diverse points of view felt they had made serious compromises in order to reach a common agreement.

Points included in the statement were: (1) there was unity in rejecting all unjust discrimination; (2) there were widely divergent views on apartheid among the groups; (3) no Christian should be excluded from any church on the grounds of race or color; (4) there are no scriptural grounds for the prohibition of mixed marriages; (5) damage to family life is one deplorable result of migrant labor; (6) objection to coloured people's participation in Parliament was unfounded. (Indians and Africans were not mentioned as voters or possible members of Parliament.)

The South African government saw the Cottesloe statement as supporting unacceptable changes and immediately denounced it. In the end, the tentative compromise of Cottesloe did not become a starting point for the churches of South Africa to work together on the crisis. Rather, the government pressured churches to separate from the WCC and prohibited financial contributions to it. The DRC was urged to sever connections with other Protestant denominations in South Africa. Since the 1970s, WCC personnel have not received visas for entry into South Africa. The DRC isolation was thus reinforced.

By the 1970s, the WCC had become more active and determined in its effort to end apartheid. In 1970, the WCC Program to Combat Racism approved its first grant of $200,000, from specially raised funds, for the educational and humanitarian work of liberation movements of southern Africa. These grants immediately became controversial, not only in South Africa but in many other countries, with governments and churches, and prompted discussions about the acceptability of aid to liberation movements. There was, however, sufficient support within the WCC to continue the grants. African Christians supported the grants, and President Kaunda of Zambia has called the grants a prophetic deed which may well be seen in the future as decisive for the church's fate in southern Africa.

In 1971, the WCC voted overwhelmingly to withdraw its

funds from corporations investing or trading in South Africa, South West Africa, and the Portuguese African territories. The 250 member churches were urged "to use all their influence, including stockholder action and divestment, to press corporations to withdraw from operations in these countries." South Africa became the focal point for divestment even though the other territories mentioned had not yet become independent. Churches, particularly in the United Kingdom, the Scandinavian countries, the Federal Republic of Germany, the Netherlands, New Zealand, Australia, Canada, and the United States, undertook divestment activities and campaigns.

The All Africa Conference of Churches, based in Nairobi and comprising most Protestant church bodies on the continent, has given strong ideological backing to the southern African liberation movements. It has taken the position that grants to the liberation movements should not be limited to their designation for humanitarian needs only. The Conference, in continual financial difficulty itself, made some small grants to the liberation movements in the mid-1970s. These grants did not cause any controversy in Africa outside South Africa.

The British Council of Churches, through its Division of International Affairs, has also been active. The BCC recognized a special responsibility in South Africa because of British historical links with it and the key role of British companies currently operating in South Africa. The BCC issued its first report on investment in South Africa in 1973. In 1979, a new report called for economic disengagement, British participation in an international oil boycott against South Africa, and British cooperation with (or at least refraining from a veto of) any UN Security Council vote for economic sanctions against South Africa. The 1979 British Council of Churches report was banned in South Africa immediately after its publication.

British churches continue to be active on South African issues. In response to an invitation of the South African Council of Churches, a delegation of nine members visited

South Africa in September 1985. Their report, *Whose Rubicon?*, briefly examines the current scene in South Africa and reaffirms the churches' responsibility for action.

The National Council of Churches of Christ in the United States has also urged both government and private economic disengagement from South Africa. A detailed policy statement on this was approved in November 1979. An important avenue of expression for this concern is the Interfaith Center on Corporate Responsibility, in which 180 Roman Catholic orders and dioceses participate, along with seventeen Protestant denominations. The Center provides research, assistance, and the stimulus for divestment and for related stockholders' resolutions. The Center targets specific U.S. corporations for action. Divestment is a growing movement within church organizations.

Corporations

Multinational corporations do not rank high as agents of political and social change. They place great importance on stability, not change. Nevertheless, because of their presence in South Africa, multinational corporations have become a major arena of contention as the citizens of the Western world seek effective ways to oppose apartheid.

Multinational corporations operating in South Africa have faced a new threat to stability: protests by consumers and stockholders in their home countries. Banks have been a prime target because they have made loans directly to the South African government and government-controlled corporations called parastatals.[6] Such loans involve banks dealing heavily in the South African economy and in direct support of the government. Between 1974 and 1976, bank lending to South Africa tripled, reaching $7.6 billion, with U.S. banks representing about one-third of the total. Many campaigns have been waged to encourage U.S. corporations and banks operating in South Africa to use their influence to bring about changes in that society. From 1977 through

1979, a number of major U.S. lenders to South Africa changed their policies, often in response to those campaigns, either withdrawing altogether, stopping future lending, or specifying that they would make no additional loans to enterprises in support of apartheid policies and discriminatory practices.[7] Loans are mentioned here as part of the catalogue of international pressures on South Africa. Recent developments in the field are discussed in the next chapter.

In 1972, a series of articles in England by Adam Raphael on the reprehensible labor policies of many British firms operating in South Africa aroused considerable public concern. This concern was taken up by the Labour government then in power in the United Kingdom. The result was a Code of Conduct in Industry and Commerce, which was followed by a number of other codes.

In early 1977, Rev. Leon Sullivan, a black minister from Philadelphia who is Director of the Opportunities Industrialization Center and a member of the board of the General Motors Corporation, set forth six principles to guide U.S. corporations operating in South Africa. These ask for: (1) nonsegregation of races in all facilities, (2) equal and fair employment practices for all employees, (3) equal pay for equal work, (4) programs to train blacks for skilled positions, (5) increases in the number of blacks in supervisory positions, and (6) improvements outside the work environment in housing, transportation, schooling, and other aspects of living conditions. The principles also include a responsibility to negotiate with black labor unions.

In June 1977, the Council of Ministers of the European Economic Community (EEC) announced a code of conduct for EEC companies which included urging companies to recognize black trade unions and to bargain collectively with them. The EEC takes no role in monitoring the effectiveness of its code.

The campaign to improve the status of blacks in the workplace has resulted in a number of such codes, perhaps as many as twenty. These codes have remained controversial among the opponents of apartheid, because they do not deal with the basic problem of the sharing of political power. The codes are seen by many to be a distraction from the main issue and a substitute for facing up to that issue.

A Case History

International pressure on South Africa can be effective.

On November 26, 1981, forty-four men who called themselves rugby players belonging to the "Ancient Order of Froth Blowers" landed in the Seychelles on a commercial flight from South Africa. Their intentions were disclosed when customs officials found guns beneath toys the Froth Blowers had "brought for poor children." These mercenaries had come to take over the government of the Seychelles. Under whose auspices they came has not been proven, but many persons suspect the South African government.

After the discovery of the hidden weapons, the men were able to escape from the airport by hijacking an Air India plane. In South Africa, five men were charged with kidnapping, a lesser offense than hijacking in South Africa, and thirty-nine were released.

South Africa signed the 1970 Hague Convention, which requires that hijackers be prosecuted or extradited. The United States, Britain, France, West Germany, Italy, Japan, and Canada have all agreed to end air links with countries breaching the Hague Convention. This sanction has been invoked against Afghanistan for failure to act in the case of a hijacked Pakistani plane.

The United States and other Western countries expressed concern, apparently with some vigor, to South Africa for its failure to comply with the Hague Convention and pointed out the inevitable consequences if the hijackers were not prosecuted.

On January 4, 1982, South African authorities acted against the entire group of mercenaries, charging them all with hijacking. They were convicted and jailed.

Evaluation

A few of the main international pressures for change have been mentioned here. There is a great diversity of pressures, all united in expressing international distaste for apartheid. The award of the Nobel Peace Prize to Bishop Tutu is, in part, a political statement of protest, as is a vote at the UN for sanctions, or the boycott of participation in the Commonwealth Games in Scotland in July 1986. Are these and other pressures effective in promoting useful change in South Africa?

The U.S. policy of constructive engagement is based on the opinion that pressures such as the above are not effective. However, constructive engagement is itself an attempt to use other tools to bring change. It can only be deplored that it has been so lacking in results.

There are those who claim that any international pressure is counterproductive. The official South African position rejects all international pressure. As just one of many possible examples, State President P. W. Botha said in his address at the adjournment of Parliament on June 19, 1985: "The international community should be in no doubt with regard to South Africa's resolve and ability to maintain itself at home, now and in the future. We can solve our problems without international meddling. . . .

"Some of them [Western governments] say they find our policies abhorrent. Well, we find their double standards and opportunistic policies abhorrent. . . .

". . . no self-respecting nation can allow any other country, large or small, to dictate how it should be governed."[8]

Perhaps P. W. Botha "protests too much." It is clear that some international protests can be shown to have specific results. One is reported above. The sports boycott has definitely created more opportunities for black athletes to participate in racially integrated sports and thousands of persons to attend sporting events as part of an integrated audience. A similar statement can be made about the boycott of and by entertainers. The refusal of the international community to accept passports from "independent" home-lands has caused South Africa to issue travel documents for these "stateless" persons. The squatter community of Crossroads would have been eliminated years ago except for international protest. There are numerous examples.

It is difficult to determine cause and effect for major changes. The new Parliament giving coloureds and Indians their first direct representation in national government is seen widely, even in South Africa, as further institutionalization of racism. The Parliament is racist both in its composition and in the omission of black Africans. Is this "reform" in response to pressure? The pass laws were under attack for decades. When they were dropped, P. W. Botha said that the pass laws were "outdated and too costly."[9]

Even P. W. Botha's protestations make it clear that he is well aware of international pressures. Such pressures are essential. They give hope to the oppressed. They give notice to the oppressor that he is being watched and is condemned. They raise the consciousness of the world to the evils of racism, not just in South Africa but everywhere. They set a context within which corporate values become important and are discussed. The protests do cause change in South Africa. The change may not be the change sought, but it will be promoted as "reform" because of the protest. That aids in creating a state of flux within which more change will occur, more change will be expected, and more pressure will be mounted to force more change.

A specific tool for change which receives a great deal of attention around the world, particularly in the United States, Western Europe, and South Africa, is divestment. Divestment/disinvestment and economic pressures for change are the subject of the next chapter.

7

Economic Pressure for Change

Each trade agreement, each bank loan, each
new investment is another brick in the wall
of our continued existence.
—John Vorster[1]

South Africa's first priority is to stop boycotts
imposed against it by Western trading partners.
—R. F. Botha[2]

Our land is burning and bleeding, so I call on the
international community to apply punitive sanctions
against this Government to help us establish a new
South Africa—nonracial, democratic, participatory
and just.
—Bishop Desmond Tutu[3]

In her first interview with a South African newspaper in more than a decade, Mrs. Winnie Mandela
called on the world to impose "immediate and total
sanctions" on the Pretoria Government.
—*The Times* (London)[4]

I believe that disinvestment and sanction are amongst
the last measures to use; even if in advocating them I
have to go to jail, I plead for them, and I'll take the
consequences for the sake of the future of our land.
—Dr. C. F. Beyers Naudé[5]

Definitions of Economic Pressure

The vocabulary for various types of economic actions has not been specific in the United States or elsewhere. In the first edition of *South Africa: Challenge and Hope,* published in 1982, all anti-apartheid economic activity was discussed under the label of divestment, the term in general use at that time. Within that definition, the American Friends Service Committee stated its position favoring economic disengagement for all individuals, organizations, and corporations from all profit-making in South Africa.

As the campaign picked up in intensity for individuals, universities, pension funds, and many others to sell stocks and bonds of companies doing business in South Africa, divestment tended to narrow in meaning to the sale of such stocks and bonds.

The withdrawal of corporation business activities in South Africa then became generally known as disinvestment, particularly in the anti-apartheid movement and in business circles where corporations faced stockholders' pressure to withdraw from South Africa.

As more and more United States companies "moved out" of South Africa, it became clear that there was a difference of vocabulary about what the anti-apartheid activists were urging and what companies were doing under the label of disinvestment.

The problem came to a sharp focus with the action of the Coca-Cola Company in September 1986. At that time, Coca-Cola announced that it was in the process of "disinvestment" from South Africa. Coke's plan was to sell all of its holdings in South Africa, primarily soft-drink bottling and distribution operations. Coke's brands, however, would continue to be sold by the new South African owners, who would import Coca-Cola syrup concentrate.

Not only anti-apartheid activists questioned Coke's claim to disinvestment. The *Atlanta Journal* editorialized: "Divestment [note terminology] Coca-Cola style is an anomaly, maybe even a misnomer . . . The firm will sacrifice little or nothing of the South African market share or profitability."

Beeld, a Johannesburg newspaper, put it even more sharply: "What a wonderful gesture—hitting out with one hand while continuing to collect money with the other!"

Coca-Cola, and much of the corporate world, seems to see disinvestment as withdrawal of capital, while AFSC and much of the anti-apartheid movement see disinvestment as total economic disengagement.

In an attempt to clarify meanings and to separate types of economic actions, the following definitions will be used here:

Divestment is the sale of shares of stock or bonds of corporations doing business in South Africa.

Disinvestment is the withdrawl of all capital assets from South Africa. (This term has been used commonly in the anti-apartheid movement to encompass broader forms of corporate withdrawl from South Africa.)

Economic disengagement is the termination of all profit-making activities, including the sale of products or distribution of goods and services (directly or through third-party arrangements), franchising, collection of royalties, consultant arrangements, and such, in addition to withdrawal of all capital assets.

Sanctions are the prohibition by a nation or group of nations of selected or total economic interchange with South Africa.

Selective purchasing and *boycott* are essentially the same, refusing to buy from or sell to South Africa selected products or all products. *Selective purchasing* often refers to the policy of U.S. city, county, and state governments in refusing to purchase goods or services from U.S. corporations which operate in South Africa. *Boycott,* of course, also includes consumer refusal to buy products of U.S. companies operating in South Africa.

Economic Pressures Increase

Economic pressure for political change in South Africa has been advocated by many governments. Citizens of North America and Western Europe have exerted pressure for economic actions on their compatriots, their governments, the European Economic Community, and corporations doing business in South Africa. Third World governments have worked through the British Commonwealth, the Organization of African Unity, and the United Nations for mandatory economic sanctions. These pressures are growing and enlisting more support, but they remain highly controversial.

The tempo of the drive for economic action against South Africa has stepped up as violence in South Africa has increased. The city of Madison, Wisconsin, passed the first selective purchasing law in 1976, but only in the last couple of years have large cities such as San Francisco, New York, and Philadelphia followed suit.

The drive for divestment has received the most attention. The Mitchell Investment Management company of Cambridge, Massachusetts, reported on May 23, 1986, that restrictions on investment in South Africa now affect "over $220 billion." This represents assets "of 19 states, 68 cities and counties, and 131 colleges and universities." This does not include the numerous divestments of churches and church organizations, labor unions, private pension funds, and other groups. Many individuals have sold shares of stocks of U.S. companies doing business in South Africa.

THREE DAYS IN MAY

Rohm and Haas Co., the huge Philadelphia chemical company, said yesterday that it would sell its South African subsidiary and end operations there because of poor business prospects.

Rohm and Haas thus joins the ranks of about

four dozen U.S. companies that have left South Africa in the last 18 months.
—Philadelphia *Inquirer,* May 22, 1986

Pennwalt Corp. has sold its interest in a small South African company and closed two service offices there to avoid conflicts with its shareholders, spokesman Lawrence Woodward said. "Those operations were so tiny that we didn't see the need to jeopardize future relations with investors over them," he said.
—Philadelphia *Inquirer,* May 23, 1986

General Motors Corp., pressured for years by apartheid foes to stop vehicle sales to the South African police and military, has cut off the sales, company chairman Roger B. Smith yesterday told the company's shareholders at GM's meeting. . . .

Smith's announcement represented a sharp break with GM's decade-long stance: that refusing to supply the white regime's armed forces and police could cause GM's expulsion from the country, where it has 200 dealers and 3,500 workers.

GM argued this point as recently as five weeks ago in proxy materials mailed to shareholders.
—Philadelphia *Inquirer,* May 24, 1986

Britain banned the import of all South African gold coins, including the recently issued Protea, Foreign Secretary Sir Geoffrey Howe said. Britain, along with many other countries, prohibited imports of South Africa's best-known gold coin, the Krugerrand, last year. Pretoria's recent issue of the Protea was widely seen as an attempt to circumvent the ban.
—Philadelphia *Inquirer,* May 24, 1986

Disinvestment is a rapidly growing form of economic pressure. Only six U.S. companies left South Africa in 1983 and seven in 1984.[6] Mitchell reports that fifty-six companies withdrew their operations from South Africa in 1984 and 1985. The two companies reported above are among those which have quit South Africa since the Mitchell report. The tempo picked up in 1986 with fifteen announcements of corporate withdrawal in the ten weeks between the middle of August and the end of October. After all of its protest against curtailment of South African involvement, even General Motors announced a five-year plan for selling out to South Africans. Corporate giants such as AT&T have made concessions to public pressure. Although AT&T will continue to supply long-distance phone service to South Africa, it is phasing out the purchase of precious metals from South Africa, has cut off computer sales, and refuses to provide special long-distance phone service such as 800 numbers.[7]

The increased economic pressure on South Africa has been the result of the effort of literally thousands of dedicated volunteer activists. College students have put particular emphasis on persuading college and university trustees to act. Activists have been well informed and encouraged by national church and civic organizations which keep the public posted with accurate, timely facts. The Interfaith Center on Corporate Responsibility in New York City (see Chapter 6) and the Investors Responsibility Research Center in Washington have tracked U.S. corporation investments and activities in South Africa. NARMIC of the American Friends Service Committee in Philadelphia has done extensive research, chiefly in the computer sector and on arms-embargo issues. In New York City the American Committee on Africa and in Washington TransAfrica and the Washington Office on Africa have followed the legislative and administrative side of action on South Africa and, in addition to lobbying, have initiated and supported many demonstrations and protests. Many religious organizations, including, among others, Catholic, Lutheran, Episcopalian, and Quaker (see the Appendix for the American Friends Service Committee policy statement), as well as the National Council of

Churches, have encouraged divestment and other kinds of anti-apartheid activity.

Bank Loans Critical

The South African economy and the government are dependent on international loans. Such loans by U.S. banks have been pinpointed as targets by activists in this country. As a result, banks have been, for the most part, more selective: they limit the purposes for which they are willing to loan money. However, following the imposition of a state of emergency by South Africa in July 1985, the international banks, reportedly led by U.S. banks, united in September to refuse to "roll over," to renegotiate, loans to South Africa coming due at that time. Such renegotiation has always been automatic in the past. About $14 billion was involved. South Africa immediately clamped a moratorium on repayment of all international loans. In negotiations with the banks, South Africa attempted unsuccessfully to get a five-year postponement on repayments. Six months of negotiations resulted in an agreement with the banks providing for a 5 percent payment on April 15, 1986, of all debt due by then and an extension of other debt to June 30, 1987. Although direct cause and effect are not demonstrable, or at least not proved, it is worth noting that the state of emergency was lifted on March 7 and the agreement with the banks was reached on March 24.

Along with the U.S. divestment and disinvestment movement, there are numerous national boycotts of South African products throughout Western Europe, ranging from Krugerrands to coal and fresh fruit. Boycotts are also used in South Africa, where blacks have demonstrated their economic power by boycotting white merchants in a number of localities.

South African Economic Problems

All these uses of economic leverage for change are taking place within the context of a South African economy in recession and under stress. At the end of April 1986, inflation for the preceding twelve months was 18.6 percent, as compared with 15.8 percent for the same period of 1984–85, according to the South African Central Statistical Services.[8] Unemployment is increasing, for the first time hitting whites, and is as high as 50 percent for blacks in some urban areas. This is in addition to the chronic unemployment and underemployment in the homelands. Drought has crippled agricultural production for several successive years, and South Africa continued to import corn from Zimbabwe in 1986 even after the drought ended in most of southern Africa. The gross domestic product fell by 1 percent in 1985.[9] Retail sales hit a five-year low in December 1985.[10]

A University of Pretoria study estimated that the economic loss due to "unrest" from September 1984 through 1985 was about $70 million. The cost of the war on the Namibian front was more than that, and the defense budget for 1986–87 has been increased by more than 19 percent, as has the budget for education, another result of "unrest." The South African unit of currency, the Rand, once worth $1.40, has declined steadily in value and hit new lows of near $0.35 in June 1986.

Immigration and emigration often serve as indicators of economic and political stability. South Africa recruits white immigrants. In 1985, as usual, more whites moved into South Africa than left. However, emigration for 1985 was 33.3 percent higher than in 1984, and immigration was 40 percent lower.[11] In 1986, for the first time, more whites emigrated than immigrated. An increasing number of skilled professionals are leaving.[12]

Gold is the wild card in the South African economy. The price of gold is not very susceptible to international manipulation, but that price has more to do with the pressures within the South African economy than sanctions or corporate economic disengagement. As a rough rule of thumb, when the price of gold is at or below $300 per ounce, South Africa is in trouble. When the price is at or over $400 per ounce, the economy has a powerful support. A $10 per ounce increase in the price of gold nets South Africa about $200 million. Thus, the approximately $70 per ounce increase in the price of gold in 1986 netted South Africa double the $700 million estimated to be lost in exports by the U.S. imposition of sanctions. Increases in the price of gold tend to benefit the white population far more than the black. Dependence on gold is a specialized problem for South Africa over which it has little control.

Arguments Against Economic Pressure

Divestment merits special attention because it involves a large number of U.S. citizens in the moral dilemmas of South African society. While most people in the United States do not eat South African lobster tails or buy Krugerrands, they do profit directly or indirectly from the economy of South Africa. They may own stock in companies that do business there, may be employed by or members of institutions that hold such stocks, may receive benefits from pension funds that hold stock in companies with South African investments, or may have accounts in banks that make loans to South Africa. U.S. trade with South Africa, both imports and exports, helps the U.S. economy, and few Americans are entirely outside this system of relationships.

Those opposed to divestment cite this economic involvement as negating the purpose of divestment. They also point out that someone else buys the divested stock or bonds, so there is no change in the overall picture of stock ownership. However, holding stock related to profit in South Africa or the sale of such stock is a political statement. It is a statement understood in this country and in South Africa.

Involvement in apartheid is a continuum of complicity. At the worst end of the continuum is total support for apartheid; at the other end is total rejection of any benefit from it. The sale of stock profiting one from business in South Africa is clearly a movement away from involvement in apartheid and toward freedom from it.

One argument against outside imposition of economic

pressure on South Africa is that such action will bring increased—in fact, greatest—hardship to those who are already suffering, the blacks. However, South African blacks often quote Chief Albert Luthuli:

> Economic boycott of South Africa will entail undoubted hardships for Africans. We do not doubt that. But if it is a method which shortens the day of bloodshed, the suffering to us will be a price we are willing to pay. In any case, we suffer already, our children are often undernourished, and on a small scale, so far, we die at the whim of a policeman.[13]

Constant suffering and continued uncertainty, according to many blacks, make additional suffering almost irrelevant and even welcome, if the right change can be brought about by it. The majority of blacks urge divestment and disinvestment, stressing their willingness to take the consequences.

Some Africans oppose divestment because their marginal existence makes the loss of a job a catastrophe for their families. The government encourages this opposition, and some leaders such as Lucy Mvubelo, General Secretary of the National Union of Clothing Workers, have been given wide exposure in South Africa and abroad speaking against divestment.

The most outspoken African on the anti-sanctions platform is Chief Mangosuthu Gatsha Buthelezi, head of the KwaZulu homeland. He is literally "on the platform," having visited the United States and a number of European countries in addition to making frequent appearances before thousands of Zulus. His message is that Africans will suffer most from economic sanctions. He has little support outside the white community and his tribal group. (The role of Chief Buthelezi is discussed in Chapter 10. Also see the Botha-Slabbert interview in the Appendix.)

There is a long list of black leaders and organizations advocating economic pressure, as well as the two leading nonracial groups, the United Democratic Front and the South

African Council of Churches. Church leaders such as Bishop Tutu, Allan Boesak, and Beyers Naudé, along with all other South Africans who advocate economic sanctions, risk imprisonment by doing so. The liberation groups—SWAPO, ANC, and PAC—all endorse economic sanctions and have done so since they were first organized. The frontline states have endorsed sanctions, even though they recognize the problems they would cause them. The various South African political, social, and student Black Consciousness groups endorse sanctions.

It isn't easy for those who have seen suffering, malnutrition, and starvation in South Africa and in other parts of the world to advocate a policy that might unintentionally add to the unemployed. It is possible that withdrawal of some foreign firms from complicity in the system of apartheid would have this effect. However, withdrawal frequently only changes the management. Loss of a job can, in South Africa, result in a worker and his family being deported ("endorsed out") to an impoverished "homeland," where earning a livelihood is practically impossible. Thus advocacy of divestment, even if it is seen only as a symbolic gesture, carries moral obligations to help South African organizations such as the SACC, SAIRR, Quaker Service, and other church relief agencies to cope with any "new" victims of apartheid.

An argument against disengagement frequently put forward by white South Africans is that liberalizing change can come to South Africa with rapid economic growth. Such growth, with the stable base it requires, can be assured only if foreign investments remain steady and secure. There is clearly some truth to this; in most societies it is easier for people to find ways to include previously excluded groups in jobs, housing, income growth, and other benefits when the economy is expanding rather than unstable or contracting. But the record of South Africa on this point is not convincing. With the strong economic growth of the past three decades, apartheid has not lessened; it has in many ways become harsher. Economic growth has not brought the social changes expected by its advocates.

American corporations argue that they are doing good by remaining in South Africa. Signatories to the Sullivan code of conduct (see Chapter 6) report having spent $158 million for social improvement for blacks. Coca-Cola set up a South African foundation with $10 million and Mobil established a foundation with about $20 million.[14] American corporations claim to be pacesetters in fair employment practices in South Africa. The anti-apartheid activists assess these efforts as, at best, making apartheid more comfortable and, at worst, assisting the South African government in developing a larger group of blacks with a stake in the status quo. These corporate gifts and practices do not address the fundamental structure of apartheid.

President Reagan and Secretary of State Shultz claim that disengagement would leave the United States with no further leverage within South Africa. It is difficult to take this argument seriously in view of the fact that in a number of countries, such as Angola, the United States has been able to apply considerable leverage with little or no assistance from resident U.S. business. Also, the argument assumes that the United States has effective leverage in South Africa now, a questionable assumption when one looks for the results of that leverage.

Another argument opposing disengagement is that if U.S. companies withdraw, others will replace them, possibly with worse treatment for black workers. From a moral standpoint, one should not continue to follow the wrong course to keep someone else from doing the same thing. While the replacement by others is possible, the reasoning underestimates the psychological impact of U.S. withdrawal on other foreign investors. Indeed, the agitation for disengagement is stronger in Europe than it is in the United States.

Some even argue that the ending of foreign investment would increase the likelihood of war; thus, those who propose disengagement are accused of "favoring violence." The premise for this argument is that opportunities for increased jobs and income for blacks come through increased investment and industrialization. If such opportunities are not provided, it is said, there would be more unemployed, starving blacks in both the bantustans and the African townships around cities. At the same time, it is believed that Afrikaners would be forced into a greater siege mentality and become even less willing to make concessions. The result, the argument goes, would be civil war. Even if the black majority does eventually gain power through this process, the system of production would be in shambles and people would be worse off than ever. Those who take this view often overlook the form of civil war that already exists, granted that a full-scale civil war would be much worse. Violence is currently high, with both sides armed and increasingly so (see Chapter 4). Sabotage, major protests, and disruptions are rising sharply and will inevitably become even more prevalent unless the apartheid system is abandoned.

The government has created many barriers to foreign disengagement. In addition to stringent laws prohibiting its advocacy in South Africa, regulations practically embargo the repatriation of capital from the country if corporations elect to withdraw. Assets must go into Rands to purchase state bonds that mature in seven to fifteen years. Only the interest may be taken out of the country. Corporations may get around this through the transfer by sale of their enterprise on the international stock exchange (assuming they can find a satisfactory buyer). Alternatively, they can license a subsidiary South African business entity to continue their operations. Some firms are using the license method. Local workers in the South African Firestone plant are reported to be very unhappy with the corporation's decision to license a South African company whose personnel policies are retrogressive. Other companies are moving their registry to Bermuda to escape pressure by technically not being European or American.

American firms are sounding out government officials on

the possibility of compensation for anticipated losses should they withdraw. A French business report early in 1982 suggested that French companies could safely operate in South Africa for only five more years. After that, financial risks would become too great.

It is understandable that corporation leaders are vexed by the issues involved with doing business in South Africa. Perhaps Flora Lewis had an encouraging message for them. She wrote: "The main reason for sanctions should be understood as our own need to show support for those who fight for dignity and decency. This is required for Western self-respect."[15]

Arguments for Economic Pressure

Many arguments for economic disengagement and for sanctions against South Africa are put in terms of disrupting its economy effectively enough to cause the government to change its policy of apartheid. Conversely, many argue against sanctions on the ground that they are not effective. Change is occurring in South Africa. Some of it is helpful and some is not. What change has come about because of economic pressure? Effectiveness is difficult to predict or assure or, in this case, even to assess.

A good case can be made that apartheid is costly to South Africa's economy and that the country's growth and prosperity would be significantly improved if apartheid were abolished. Apartheid, with its inferior education, restrictive labor practices, and severely limited political advancement for blacks, prevents the development of skilled workers and affluent consumers needed by the South African economy. Nonetheless, apartheid continues. Apartheid is motivated by more than profitability. Even if it could be conclusively demonstrated that profits would be higher without it, many white South Africans still would hold to the beliefs which underlie apartheid. It is not clear that an economy, particularly one as strong as South Africa's, suffers in the long run from having investment and trade withdrawn. The government may become increasingly able to resist outside pressure as it is forced to rely less and less on outside economic support. Arguments for economic sanctions that are based solely on effectiveness are not the strongest arguments.

Many concerned people argue for selective disinvestment and sanctions as being more effective and easier to implement. They suggest that companies that fail to live up to the Sullivan principles, banks directly supporting the South African government, or companies involved in military and security operations should become targets of disinvestment. Oil, because of its importance to the economy and South Africa's lack of an internal supply, is frequently seen as a prime target for sanctions and has been discussed at the United Nations for more than twenty years.

These examples are all valid means for protest and pressure for change. However, the complexity of the changing economic scene makes it very difficult to distinguish fairly between companies with disparate operations. Further, it is not clear that the impact would be as significant as that of more comprehensive action.

Others suggest another selective approach. They point out that investments in institutions specifically directed at black development support strength in that community and bring change. While this idea holds clear merit, it is difficult to identify circumstances where such support could be effective. Under the laws on land and holding titles, blacks in South Africa can provide little security in exchange for loans to begin businesses. Few U.S. banks, for example, have provided capital for the African bank or insurance company established by the African Chamber of Commerce (NAF-COC). Few are offering soft loans for African entrepreneurs wishing to get started. What does seem clear is that a time will come when investment, loans, and other forces of economic engagement and support will be terribly important in helping to build a new South African society based on equality of opportunity and justice for all of its citizens.

A strong argument for divestment and disengagement is the message—moral, political, and economic—that such action communicates both to the current South African government and business communities and to the black people of South Africa. To the ruling minority the message would be: We are giving up the profits we might gain from your reprehensible system of racist oppression.

To the oppressed majority, the message would be of solidarity. We would be saying that we shall take as strong an economic action as is possible to help change the system of oppression.

Leon Sullivan, originator of the Sullivan code of conduct, approves a progression from codes and partial divestment to more comprehensive actions. In 1980 he said: "I will be supporting selective divestments against American companies that do not cooperate with the principles, and who fail to comply favorably with their implementation. I will be 'calling for' and urging strong U.S. government action against them, including tax penalties, sanctions and loss of government contracts. And, *if change does not come fast enough* [Sullivan's emphasis], I will consider stronger measures, including total divestment and ultimately total embargo of all American exports and imports to and from South Africa."[16]

By 1986 Leon Sullivan was attempting to obtain $100 billion in divestment pledges to be implemented if apartheid didn't end by May 31, 1987.[17]

It is time that Britain stopped wringing its hands and uttering ritual condemnations. The policy of urging peaceful change while providing South Africa with the loans and the trade and foreign investment on which its loathsome Government depends has always smacked of hypocrisy.

It must be clear by now, even to Mrs. Thatcher and Sir Geoffrey Howe, that South Africa cannot be sweet-talked into change.

—*The Observer* (London)[18]

Finally, the strongest argument in favor of disengagement and divestment is a moral one. Quaker leader John Woolman gave good advice back in the eighteenth century: "May we look upon our treasures, the furniture of our houses, and our garments, and try whether the seeds of war have nourishment in these our possessions."[19]

To be engaged in making a profit of any sort in South Africa is to be making a profit from an immoral and unjust system of oppression. The same argument is true for other economic relationships, such as the purchase of South African products.

All businesses in South Africa, whether or not they operate under the Sullivan principles or invest in black enterprises, are inhibited in openly opposing the political, legal, and social framework of apartheid. They are actually coopted by the South African government and, under some conditions, become part of the enforcement process along with the police and the Army. The National Key Points Act requires companies to take security precautions, such as storing weapons and communications equipment and training and organizing reserve units to guard national "key points" against any protesters or other interference. The large U.S. enterprises involved in such fields as energy, computers, and electronics come under the definition of "key point": "any place or area so important that its loss or damage, disruption or immobilization may prejudice the Republic or wherever [the Minister of Defense] considers it necessary for the safety of the Republic."

Thus U.S. enterprises are pulled into the South African defense mechanisms and are involved in supporting the system. Moreover, by proclaiming an emergency, the government can order any company in South Africa to produce what the country needs for defense. A company producing passenger cars may find itself producing tanks, jeeps, or armored cars. The blueprints for such retooling are already in hand. It is impossible in South Africa not to be involved in the apartheid system. Therefore, a decision about divestment, disengagement, or sanctions is made finally in terms of the morality of involvement in apartheid.

At some point one is compelled to abandon attempts to balance the good that can be done despite remaining linked to the South African economy with the harm that may be done by withdrawing. Cutting the link to apartheid is the moral basis for the action of many individuals, organizations, and governmental units in deciding to sell the stock of corporations doing business in South Africa. This moral step conveys, in the strongest possible terms, one's abhorrence for the system of apartheid and complicity with it. Critics of divestment and disinvestment have complained of a resulting separation of people. Cutting economic links need not separate anyone from any of the people of South Africa. There is a distinction between people and a system which is detrimental to them all.

Labor Unions

"The entire South African economy is based on black labor. Blacks make up 90% of the entire mining workforce—a critical source of South African capital—and 75% of the manufacturing workforce—the backbone of the economy. Black workers produce over half of all the country's textiles, metals, rubber, chemicals, machinery, paper, plastics, wood, and food products. They account for 72% of all South African workers . . ."[20]

The potential for economic pressure from organized black labor is clear. Over the years there have been sporadic strikes by black workers, although such strikes were always illegal and strikers were usually fired immediately. A change in the law in 1979 made it possible for black unions to register, i.e. be legally recognized, and to call a legal strike after exhausting the procedures for settlement. The first legal strike by an African union was that of the National Union of Mineworkers in 1984.

Black workers were organized before 1979, and some employers dealt with them as a matter of practicality, but the agreements were not enforceable in law. Some black unions still operate without registration, largely because registration involves disclosure about leaders, membership, and finances. There is an understandable hesitancy about how much any black organization in South Africa wishes to tell the government. Fifty-one trade union officers were detained in 1984.[21] South Africa has not released statistics but news sources agreed that hundreds of union leaders were detained in 1986.

The first successful, widespread job action as political protest sponsored by the unions came in November 1984 when 800,000 workers stayed at home to protest the use of troops for police duty in the townships.

After months of negotiations, South Africa's largest federation of unions was formed in November 1985. The Congress of South African Trade Unions (COSATU) has 500,000 members. It is a combination of the Federation of South African Trade Unions (FOSATU) and the National Union of Mineworkers (NUM), which withdrew its 100,000 black members from the Council of Unions of South Africa (CUSA). COSATU is predominantly black in membership but nonracial in both membership and philosophy. Nelson Mandela is the honorary president of NUM.

CUSA still has 150,000 members and takes the position that union leadership must be African, as does the much smaller Azanian Congress of Trade Unions.

A fourth federation is the Trade Union Council of South Africa, with 350,000 members, some of whom are white, but most are coloured.

The white federation, with 100,000 members, is the South African Confederation of Labor.

On May 1, 1986, Chief Buthelezi and Inkatha launched the United Workers Union of South Africa (UWUSA). Although 70,000 persons were reported to be at the public inauguration of UWUSA in Durban, its membership is unknown. Chief Buthelezi, called by the press "the guest

speaker," committed the new union to working against disinvestment and in cooperation with the labor-law machinery of South Africa. A COSATU meeting in Durban the
same day was attended by 150,000 persons (press estimates
of both crowds).

Any of these unions could spark economic pressure, but
COSATU, with its thirty-three unions, has been taking the
lead. Government leaders accuse COSATU of being in league
with the United Democratic Front and ANC.

In 1986, COSATU was the major force behind the workers' declaration of May 1 as a public holiday. It became South
Africa's biggest "stayaway," with an estimated 1,500,000
workers taking the day off. More than 200,000 people attended rallies across the country. It was a day of peaceful
protest. Most employers took the position of no pay and no
penalties.

On the tenth anniversary of the Soweto uprising, June 16,
1986, COSATU cooperated with the United Democratic
Front and the National Education Crisis Committee in another massive, national "stayaway." Strict government censorship made the gathering and dissemination of news difficult, but from the observation of empty commuter trains
and "no show" buses for the lack of drivers, it is assumed
that the June 16 demonstration surpassed that of May 1. There
was no attempt by the authorities to get people to work,
and most employers again opted for no pay and no penalties.

The late United Mine Workers president John L. Lewis,
a forceful American labor leader, said that you cannot mine
coal with a bayonet. This was at the time of a strike when
it was threatened that the National Guard would take over
the mines. The bayonet is not a useful tool for many other
jobs either. South Africa's black unions are politically ori-
ented and strengthening their organizations, confident that
the work they do cannot be done by the government forces.
They have flexed their muscles peacefully. Their existence

in the midst of their own state of oppression creates economic pressure. The action has just begun on this front.

Summary

In spite of the extensive poverty within the black community in South Africa, the racist discrimination in pay scales and job placement, and the vast economic problems of the homelands, South Africa's basic problem is not economic but political. The most important problem is the just sharing of political power.

However, the economic and political problems are interrelated. The South African economy cannot support recognized needs of better black education and housing, for example, in part because of the cost of war on the border of Namibia and in part because of international economic sanctions. The economy is in recession with double-digit inflation. The demands of increasingly better organized black labor unions combine economic and political objectives. The economic position of whites unites many of them in an effort to maintain the political status quo as a defense of economic privilege.

Much of the drive of divestment and economic disengagement in the United States and Europe is based on the moral position that profits from apartheid are unacceptable. But there is a strong, and perhaps numerically larger, component of the advocates of economic sanctions who believe weakening the economy weakens the extent of economic privilege and creates an instability within which political change becomes possible. The holders of these two points of emphasis unite in seeing economic sanctions against South Africa as a strong political statement against apartheid and for the political rights of blacks.

The South African economy is an important battlefield in the confrontation for liberation.

8

Confronting the Tenacity
of Power

At the end of the day I fear that the drama can only
be brought to its climax in one of two ways—
through the selective brutality of terrorism or the
impartial horrors of war.
—Kenneth Kaunda[1]

This chapter considers nonviolence as a strategy for change as part of the challenge and hope of South Africa.

People do not easily surrender their power or the privilege it brings them. Indeed, the perquisites of privilege are regarded by those who hold them, not as a coat that can be taken off and generously given away, but as the very substance of cultural heritage and values which make life worth living. This is all the more true in South Africa, where Afrikaners believe they have a religious mission to hold and control the land. Their determination is strengthened by the fact that they have no alternative European homeland.

The toughness of their security measures is matched by the eagerness of their argued rationalizations. A major justification is the preservation of the ethnic and cultural identities of a diversity of peoples and homelands. In a pamphlet published in January 1981 and widely circulated by the South African government, Dr. Jan S. Marais, South African economist and banker, neatly blends the long-standing government policy into the worldwide movement for self-determination:

> Throughout the world distinctive national groups are clamouring for their "national identity" and retention of their culture. . . . In South Africa, national groups are given the option of ruling themselves as independent nations. American minority groups have never been offered this option. . . . And what of the Palestinian paradox? Whilst the world refuses to recognize Transkei, a homeland is urged for the Palestinian people to "give effective expression to a people's national dignity."[2]

Various critics of the government hold a different point of view. The Christian Institute, which was banned a year later, said in 1976:

> History will judge the homelands policy of the South African Government to be a sham and a fraud designed to perpetuate white domination over the country as a whole, and to provide a pretext for arbitrarily depriving millions of black South Africans of their natural birthright of citizenship in a country whose wealth they have played a major part in creating.[3]

Despite worldwide protests and some token reforms, the government continues a policy of deportation to homelands that are limited in resources, poor in land, and already crowded with people who are unemployed and often malnourished.

The application of the principle of cultural separation to their own group—an Afrikaner-Anglo homeland more proportionate to the size of their population, i.e. 16 percent of the land instead of 87 percent—is seriously proposed only by a few extremist whites. The driving forces of industrialization and economic interdependence have gone too far to make such a solution possible, even if it were desired.

Pressure for Change

The main force for change is coming from the oppressed people. As they rise to claim their rightful human heritage, the structures of oppression are beginning to crumble. Frederick Douglass articulated the militant spirit of the anti-slavery movement in the nineteenth century in the United States. In a speech in 1857 he said:

> The limits of tyrants are prescribed by the endurance of those whom they oppress. . . . If there is no struggle there is no progress. Those who profess to favor freedom and yet depreciate agitation are men who want crops without plowing up the ground; they want rain without thunder and lightning. They want the ocean without the awful roar of its many waters.[4]

The struggle of blacks in South Africa against the domination of whites has passed through four phases: armed struggle, political resistance, nonviolent struggle, and back to armed struggle.

1. The first phase, sporadic warfare, was nearly ended by 1900.

2. In the latter part of the nineteenth century and the beginning of the twentieth, most of the resistance was political within the legal framework. The normal political practices of voting, abstaining from voting as protest, petitions, negotiations, and other such methods were used.

3. From the formation of the African National Congress in 1912, through Sharpeville in 1960, nonviolent direct action was the primary thrust of black resistance. Demonstrations, marches, sit-ins, pass burnings, civil disobedience, and other techniques not usually part of the political process marked the era.

4. Since Sharpeville, armed struggle has been seen by many blacks as a necessary tool for liberation. Armed struggle in this context includes urban guerrilla sabotage and the burning, looting, and destruction of government property,

often in the African townships. The killing of "stooges" or "sellouts" is a new and grim part of the armed struggle.

The strategies of these four periods overlap, and armed violence is used as part of a total strategy that includes political resistance and nonviolent action. New techniques may be developed, such as the already evident massive attendance at funerals of those killed in the struggle, the creation of organizations without leaders who are publicly identifiable, and consumers' boycotts. Is it possible for a fifth phase to appear with primary reliance on nonviolent noncooperation? The possibilities at this time seem dim despite continued widespread use of nonviolent techniques.

There is a great deal of experience in South Africa with nonviolence, but the proponents of armed struggle now seem to be in the majority. Many nonviolent efforts in South Africa, such as consumers' boycotts and staying away from school, are marred by violent efforts at enforcement against those persons who do not wish to participate. Other successful attempts at nonviolent protest, such as continued massive attendance at funerals of those killed by the police, or marches on prisons, are often disrupted and end in violent confrontation after police initiate the use of force.

South Africans are the main force for the creation of a more humane order. Concerned persons in other countries cannot impose a selection of strategies on those in the fray. All strategies for change are difficult in South Africa because power is extremely one-sided. With these limitations in mind, various conciliatory forces within South Africa and proposals for negotiations are worth considering. The individual moral approach and the possibilities of collective nonviolent campaigns carried on outside and inside South Africa are part of this.

These responses are appraised with the knowledge that other persons may reach different conclusions. Outsiders, although limited in influence, are freer to follow conscientious leanings because they are not direct participants in either the repression or the humiliation. People in the United States and Europe should remember that, in spite of themselves, they are involved through many linkages with exploitation in South Africa. Involvement in the movement to remove injustices is possible by breaking through silence and apathy into action.

Conciliatory Efforts

Despite the drastic confrontation of forces in South Africa, efforts of individuals and groups to cross the barriers using communication, moral suasion, and conciliation should not be dismissed. Since the South African system is based to some extent on biblical interpretation, theological and biblical arguments against apartheid may have an effect in some circles and should be stressed as a tactic and also as a means of sharing the truth. Exposure to outside thinking, insofar as it is possible, can counter narrow-mindedness and internal censorship. Many people in South Africa find themselves in the middle between the ruling group and afflicted blacks. They are strongly against apartheid, but through constraints of job, family, and temperament find it difficult to join a movement of opposition. These persons have on occasion protested the harsh actions of the authorities, helped families in distress, and given succor to persecuted individuals. Anything that can be done to reduce the fears and prejudices of white South Africans, not least those in the government, may help to bring a better future. While overtures by persons doing what they can within their limits are useful, they don't provide the main thrust against apartheid. They are valid if they promote, and do not inadvertently obstruct, the change that is needed.

In our situation in South Africa today it would be totally un-Christian to plead for reconciliation and peace before the present injustices have been removed. Any such plea plays into the hands of the

> oppressor by trying to persuade those of us who
> are oppressed to accept our oppression and to be-
> come reconciled to the intolerable crimes that are
> committed against us. That is no Christian rec-
> onciliation, it is sin. It is asking us to become ac-
> complices of the devil. No reconciliation is possi-
> ble in South Africa *without justice.*
> —The Kairos Document, signed by more
>   than 150 South African theologians and
>   other church leaders[5]

Conciliation and reconciliation have often been misunder-
stood. Nothing here is intended to suggest any form of reconciliation with apartheid. Apartheid, and all the levels of
legal and cultural "apartness" symbolized by that word, must
go. There can be no reform of, nor reconciliation with,
apartheid.

The conciliation needed in South Africa is the people-to-
people reaching across the barriers of race, ethnic groups,
and political belief. This is the process of easing, perhaps
speeding, transition. It is a way of nurturing the new society
and new institutions yet to come. It is where nonviolence
has the profound advantage over armed conflict.

Negotiation, Mediation, and Change

There is an important distinction between bridge-building
conciliation within the current structures and negotiation for
a redistribution of power. Those who work for a just peace
are eager to find ways to substitute negotiation for violence.
In a situation of great inequity such as that in South Africa,
negotiation for a new balance of power is part of the process
of change when the oppressed have gained sufficient strength
to obstruct governmental decisions and make their own decisions. Also, negotiations become meaningful when authority is challenged and the government is forced to deal

with the real leaders of the people and not those of its own choosing. Prematurely attempted, negotiation and mediation may hinder change by sidetracking the demands of those seeking political power and strengthening the hold of the ruling power. When the opposing forces are more nearly equal, negotiation becomes a pertinent method of bringing about change and finding new political forms.

It is then that third-party mediation by official international or national bodies may become important. The parties in the conflict will still be caught up in hostility and mistrust. The ruling group will still be trying to keep its hold. Each side is likely to say that it cannot possibly speak to the other. Each side may still be looking for resources, outside help, and collective will to overcome the opponent. The third party, which may be invited or may intervene, may provide an atmosphere of neutrality without ulterior motive, supportive of negotiation and compromise.

Third parties can facilitate the process of talks if they have the confidence of both sides and can move back and forth with discretion and without publicity. They can carry messages between groups not on speaking terms, convey impressions of the willingness to negotiate, and even at times suggest terms. Confidence is difficult to earn, since third parties cannot be neutral in the face of tyranny. Their sympathies and actions must be clearly on the side of the oppressed, but willingness at all times to speak to those in power can still bring openings.

The lesson of Zimbabwe illustrates these points. Over the years, many attempts at negotiation failed; the illegal UDI regime of Ian Smith was not ready to give up; the opposition forces of ZANU and ZAPU were not strong enough to gain major concessions. The UN sanctions against Southern Rhodesia were, however, one factor in changing the power relationship between blacks and whites. They gave blacks a sense of international support and encouragement while causing difficulties for the Smith government. At the stage when guerrilla forces controlled large parts of the population by night while the Rhodesian armed forces maintained sporadic control by day, the ruling group came to realize it was trying to defend a political order, namely white supremacy, which no longer existed and could not be restored.

In April 1979 in a last-minute effort to retain some power, the government held elections which were boycotted by the two liberation movements. Bishop Muzorewa, one of the African leaders who had agreed to the elections, became Prime Minister, but Smith's Rhodesian Front Party retained the major controls, giving currency to the phrase "internal settlement." The new government was not recognized by the international community and the civil war continued.

Commonwealth heads of government meeting in Zambia in August 1979 worked out the Lusaka Accord, which envisaged a process of peaceful transition to majority rule through supervised elections. In accordance with the terms of the Lusaka agreement, the British government convened a constitutional conference at Lancaster House in London in September 1979.

Among other groups, the American Friends Service Committee and Quaker Peace and Service of London were able to play a minor role in this process. Because they had maintained a relationship with liberation leaders over the years, they could facilitate communication between participants on the fringes of the very difficult negotiations which set the stage for a new order. Elections ultimately were held as a result of the 1979 talks, supervised by British authorities. The old-order leaders and their allies, including South Africa, fully expected that the government of Muzorewa would win. The balloting was carefully safeguarded by civil servants and monitored by a host of foreign correspondents and a Commonwealth Observer Group. The people showed unmistakably that the guerrilla leaders Robert Mugabe and Joshua Nkomo were their choice.

Individual Conscience and Social Change

Much religious thought and faith emphasize individual morality as the primary response to social evil. An individual may sell his or her stock in a multinational corporation operating in South Africa, because it is wrong to profit from exploitation. The pacifist refuses to participate in war. Such actions are not necessarily based on a calculation of consequences or a tally of beneficial results. By themselves these actions will not end apartheid or stop war. The moral witness says: "I do what I must do and leave the rest to God."

This personal position has validity and frequently embodies a degree of commitment that is important in a movement for social change. In South Africa courageous young whites are refusing to participate in the military. Some are going to jail, others are leaving the country. Many leaders of the End Conscription Campaign were detained in 1985–86. If such action becomes contagious and many are moved to do the same things the movement may have a political effect. It has caused churches and the government to give serious consideration to conscientious objection to war, resulting in some recognition of conscience.

A variant of the personal approach is the strategy of converting the leaders of an evil government. The thought is that if only the few responsible can be brought to see the light, then a transformation will be accomplished. Power and privilege in South Africa are held not just by a few individuals but in varying degrees by a whole class of people, defined by skin color, whose lives are inextricably bound up with the status quo. They are all children of God. They think of themselves as estimable fathers and mothers, warmhearted, generous, hardworking, courageous, and strong. The Afrikaners think they are inheritors of a noble tradition which they must protect. But they are caught in a rigid world of self-confirming action and logic which leads them to think their advantaged position is sacrosanct. Such people, however well-meaning and sincere, are not easily open to persuasion.

The hard truth is that confrontation and resistance are necessary for a reallocation of power. A few may be converted, but their transformation puts them beyond the pale of their own society—shunned, banned, or exiled. Such was the fate of the former head of the Christian Institute, Beyers Naudé, now General Secretary of the South African Council of Churches. His heroic witness will someday be vindicated, but for now it has produced but a small dent in the armor of apartheid. Individual conversions are an inspiration to many and have some cumulative effect, but oppressed people cannot be expected to wait until a large enough number of the oppressors have seen their error and embraced drastic change. The personal approach is not an adequate response to an aroused people in a desperate situation. It can readily become an excuse for inaction. Lucretia Mott, the nineteenth-century Quaker leader in the abolitionist and women's movements, said: "Any great change must expect opposition because it shakes the very foundation of privilege," and later: "We are not to wait until all are converted to pure nonresistance any more than we had to wait for all to be made antislavery in heart."[6]

Nonviolent Direct Action

The individual conscience propelled by its own inner dynamic has often moved on from a personal stand to inspire collective resistance. Participants in such group action will be faced with difficult questions. There is no sure litmus test for any action to determine the degree of physical or psychological violence that may ensue from it. Those working on a strategy for nonviolent struggle must also face the question of effectiveness, as well as the question of how the particular strategy suits their value judgment on nonviolence. Gwendolen Carter says that violence in South African society "is so pervasive that it almost ceases to be noticeable except when a well known person is affected or the circumstances are so unusual as to attract attention."[7]

In the atmosphere of spiraling violence in South Africa, it may be chimerical to look for a return to nonviolent struggle as the primary method of working for liberation. Yet such a turn could be an important key to a compassionate solution which would benefit all, whites as well as blacks.

Even as this is said it must be acknowledged that the discipline of nonviolence does not come easily. A violent reaction on the part of an affronted person is commonly seen as self-defense and an assertion of dignity. Nonviolent resistance must be much more studied and planned. Many will find it easier to fight back than to accept suffering and turn it into a challenge to the conscience of others. Rev. Allan Boesak, in his meeting with British religious leaders following his release from detention in September 1985, spoke of the "indignity of not resisting" and said that he saw creative nonviolent action as not only possible but imperative. In a nonviolent campaign, feelings of wrath ideally are transmuted into resistance which minimizes the spirit of revenge. Those already suffering are required to stand up before batons and gunfire without hurling brickbats and broken bottles at the users of armed force.

The argument of nonviolent resistance is that people, with only their bare hands, have a monopoly of moral force, even though the governing power has a monopoly of weapons of suppression. Moral force is enhanced by a movement which relies on the power of love rather than the power to kill.

The South African government presents a classic example of muscle-bound bureaucracy, bristling with arms and ideologically ill equipped to meet the challenge of massive, nonviolent noncooperation. The government has already demonstrated an inability to use its bludgeoning techniques to foreclose strikes involving even a relatively small geographic area and a relatively small number of workers. Strike actions are growing. What would happen if the black workers, servants, and farm laborers withdrew cooperation on a massive scale in a well-organized nonviolent campaign!

Is it possible that at a certain point, as Kaunda puts it, the oppressor will realize that "he is powerless, in the last resort, to prevent the inevitable, because he is trying to fight not an army but an idea, and short of exterminating a whole population he cannot bomb or blast it out of their minds"?[8]

The truth of the idea—acknowledging the humanity of thirty million people—is better served by nonviolent actions which do not deny the basic humanity of the oppressor. Will there be a moment of truth when the South African rulers find that the rigid confining fabric of apartheid is stretched so far that it breaks? Will there emerge a resolution in the highest circles to free all the South African people from bondage and devote the immense resources of South Africa to the development of all of southern Africa? It is difficult to be optimistic, but such a possibility cannot be dismissed.

The keys to successful organization of a nonviolent campaign are an awakened people and skilled leaders. All leaders must understand the use of nonviolent techniques and must be willing to suffer. They must believe that they can convince their opponents to change their ways more effectively by nonviolent action than by killing and maiming. The people must remain alert, aroused to the necessity for struggle, mobilized, disciplined to work together, and willing to forego retaliation. Three well-known South African leaders with great potential for nonviolent leadership have all died: Sobukwe of PAC and Luthuli of ANC while restricted, and Biko of the Black Consciousness Movement while in police custody. New leaders continue to develop in the squatters' movements, school boycotts, and trade unions and keep a low profile in the emerging style of organization.[9] Much of the current anti-government activity is nonviolent. The precedent of Gandhi's work, in both India and South Africa, and the Defiance Campaign led by Chief Luthuli are a part of the heritage of today's resistance movement. However, today's resistance lacks cohesion and close commitment to the goal of transforming the system without annihilating its proponents.

The evaluation of the effectiveness of acts of resistance often differs among participants and among observers. The anti-pass-laws demonstration at Sharpeville, which cost seventy lives, visibly shook the government of South Africa. Because of the deaths and the lack of change in the pass laws, the demonstration was called a failure by the liberation movement, justifying a move to guerrilla warfare. However, the guerrilla warfare on the Namibian border, which has cost thousands of lives, seems to have done little to change South Africa and is not called a failure.

The philosophy of nonviolent confrontation is based not on comparative death counts but rather on the possibility of redeeming a sick society by resisting evil and accepting suffering as necessary. The acts of confrontation and disobedience are directed against a system and not against a people. The hope is to win over the oppressors by "soul-force" or "love-force." The power and riches of the ruling groups are predicated on the coerced consent of the oppressed. If this consent is replaced by active resistance, power and privilege eventually collapse, making way for a new order to emerge.

The problem for the Church here is the way the word violence is being used in the propaganda of the State. The State and the media have chosen to call violence what some people do in the townships as they struggle for their liberation, i.e. throwing stones, burning cars and buildings and sometimes killing collaborators. But this *excludes* the structural, institutional and unrepentant violence of the State and especially the oppressive and naked violence of the police and the army. These things are not counted as violence. And even when

they are acknowledged to be 'excessive,' they are
called 'misconduct' or even 'atrocities' but never
violence. Thus the phrase 'violence in the townships' comes to mean what the young people are
doing and not what the police are doing or what
apartheid in general is doing to people.
—The Kairos Document[10]

The Challenge to Nonviolence

Those of us who call on others to practice nonviolence to
achieve radical change in South Africa recognize the challenge to nonviolent commitment and belief in that country.
The cost of the struggle in South Africa demands of those
who believe in nonviolence that they go well beyond a superficial effort to be peacemakers. It is essential to listen
carefully to black South Africans. It is a predominantly white,
unthreatened group of Americans who call upon a black,
beleaguered community to consider nonviolence. To practice nonviolence would mean to accept violence directed at
themselves, while sparing their white oppressor the death
and destruction of armed violence.

A large majority of those deeply involved in the struggle
for justice in South Africa state frankly and sincerely that
they see no alternative to widespread use of armed force. In
the face of this challenge to the nonviolent position it may
be too easy to pin one's hopes on bridge building and conciliation, personal witness, and negotiation. Experience in
the United States offers only a limited knowledge of what
it means to be committed to nonviolence to achieve fundamental, radical change on a national scale.

The struggle in this country has been different. Nonviolent movements in the United States have fought for racial
justice, for peace, and for women's rights. For the most part,
these have been confrontations in which the nation and its
leaders were pressed to live up to the country's best ideals,

to enforce its constitution, to carry out certain selective structural changes that would be consonant with the best democratic visions of the society.

Nonviolent action in the United States has generally consisted of legally sanctioned marches and other peaceful demonstrations, selective boycotts, and civil disobedience—almost always with a limited risk of either extensive jail sentences or official violence. When the participants returned home after a day, a week, or a month of such action, almost never have they had to be concerned about midnight knocks at the door, police detention without charges, being banned, lifelong imprisonment, or death.

One of the experiences with something broader and deeper came in the 1950s and 1960s when the U.S. black civil rights movement in the South confronted the state and local governments. The cruelty of police and white mobs in some situations was a small indication of what one can expect in South Africa. Demonstrators in the United States were almost always able to look to the federal government for protection against the worst assaults of violent repression. Rarely, if ever, in U.S. experience have citizens engaged in or witnessed a massive, sustained nonviolent campaign that challenged the legitimacy, authority, and political foundations of the national government. Americans are insulated against a sense of what might really be involved in such a campaign: the costs, the implications, and the furor—as well as the blessings—of such nonviolence.

In speaking responsibly of nonviolence in a situation like that in South Africa, one must be more than sounding brass and tinkling cymbal with the announcement of commitment to nonviolence in the face of the South African government's pervasive system of violent coercion. Americans must at least stretch their imaginations to try to understand the experience of others.

This country's colonial leaders chose armed rebellion as the way to break out of British domination, which in comparison to the South African situation seems gentle and beneficent. Even then there were Quakers, Mennonites, and others who paid the price with their possessions and their freedom for refusal to pay taxes or to support that war in other ways. The entrenchment and protection of the system of slavery in the law and in social and economic arrangements made radical abolitionism a dangerous vocation. To oppose slavery required in many cases a lifelong commitment to civil disobedience, a readiness to face the terrible onslaughts of mobs, and a commitment to persevere until death. Slavery was finally ended not only by heroic, nonviolent action on the part of blacks and whites but also through the bloodshed of a civil war that was primarily fought to preserve the Union. The bitter legacy of that war, which ended the institution of slavery but not racism, still plagues the United States.

There was a massive, essentially nonviolent movement for the re-creation of American society after the Civil War. Black people, with a small band of allies, were determined to press beyond slavery to create a new society. They sought to end dehumanizing white supremacy and to establish political equality.

Such a vision challenged the assumptions of white supremacy on the part of the vast majority of the nation, including the leadership of the federal government. The newly freed black community had to deal with that reality. Moreover, in Mississippi and South Carolina the former slaves were a majority, and in scores of counties throughout the southern Black Belt they were present in proportions quite similar to those in South Africa. Their numbers and their vision threatened the whites of the region, who were supported by the whites of the nation. This fundamentally nonviolent black movement, begun in the first decade after the Civil War, was betrayed and buried for half a century, largely through the force of white arms and the coercive use of white economic power. In the course of more than a decade of struggle, thousands of black persons lost their lives, and tens of thousands more were hounded out of the region. To consider the extent of that crushing, bloody repression of an essentially unarmed force seeking basic transformation of the political and economic order must surely fill Americans with a deep sense of humility and trepidation as they state a belief in nonviolence for other lands. The important point here is the realization that there are some models in U.S. society of mass, nonviolent campaigns for fundamental change. Each was born of the time and circumstance, rather than out of a spiritual commitment to nonviolence.

The one national nonviolent, revolutionary struggle that is a model to follow is that of India during the decades of Gandhi's *Satyagraha* movement. Here is an example that brings hope for a national mass, nonviolent struggle for freedom. But one must not be facile or simplistic in attempting to apply Gandhi's lessons and inspiration to South Africa.

Gandhi was not faced with an entrenched white settler population that was determined to rule India as its own homeland. The British center of power and decision making was thousands of miles away, and India was only a part of its extended colonial empire. The British government sent subalterns—brutal ones as well as humane ones—to deal with the Indian movement. In South Africa, white power is there, not nine thousand miles away, entrenched on the land that each party claims as its home. The weapons of repression are there in full supply, along with the troops.

The goals of the Indian movement, like those of similar anti-colonial struggles elsewhere, were simple: the removal of British rule. In South Africa, the problem is more complex and more explosive. While the British in India used violence, coercion, and brutality, they did not reach the South African levels of organized, repressive force.

Even though the Indian struggle was simpler, it required decades of sacrificial nonviolent action and tremendous demands on the lives of all participants. Nor was it without outbursts of violence coming from the impatience of the people. Although the struggle for independence was successful, the tragedies of the Muslim–Hindu split, the assassination of the Mahatma, and the fundamental confusion of much of the nonviolent leadership after his death show that the positive aims of a nonviolent movement are not easy to sustain.

How can there be nonviolent, transforming, compassionate action in South Africa? Has the massive commitment of life, energy, imagination, and determination that will be required to carry out a truly just revolution in South Africa been soberly, honestly considered?

South Africans have a right to ask questions about U.S. support of the government of South Africa, the U.S. reliance on violence for national security, and matters of racial and economic injustice still unsettled in the United States. South Africans have a right to ask about the failure of nonviolent action to solve these problems. It is important to hear these questions. U.S. action against apartheid may be the best response.

Those who are prepared to make an active response are challenged to carry out nonviolent acts of imaginative and symbolic disobedience against the evil of apartheid and U.S. complicity in it. The Call to Conscience Campaign of 1986 may stimulate such actions. Those nonviolent actions would not take the place of, but would be added to, the educational and lobbying work of many organizations, mass protests like the three-thousand-person African Liberation Day demonstration in Washington of May 1981, or the highly visible actions in 1985 and 1986 of the hundreds of persons arrested in front of the South African Embassy in Washington and at South African consulates around the country.

Such witness in the United States would have a much more profound effect on the movement for liberation in South Africa than any arguments for African pursuit of nonviolence. South African blacks seek a radical contribution to their cause. A strong campaign against U.S. complicity in the system would be welcome support. If South Africans are asked to consider sacrificial nonviolent struggle, the call should be authenticated by action in this country.

This leads beyond despair. Hope begins with an honest appraisal of the life that stirs within and around each person. The American revolution for equality of all persons before the law does not have to be completed before finding some way to stand in solidarity with those who seek justice and humane transformation of their society in South Africa or elsewhere.

The violence of the South African government seeking to maintain minority control and the lesser violence of the liberation groups seeking a new society will continue to challenge nonviolence. The South African government indicated its willingness to respond with lethal force against nonviolent protest during the declared emergencies of 1985–86 and earlier against nonviolent protest in Soweto in 1976 and Sharpeville in 1960.

In the traumatic experience of tragedies such as those of Soweto and Sharpeville, it is easy to overlook the fact that nonviolence is as endemic to South Africa as violence. Young white South Africans are saying no to conscription and going to prison or into exile or spending years of their lives in alternative civilian service. Church leaders have risked their lives standing between the police and attenders at funerals whom the police were trying to disperse. Winnie Mandela has ignored the law and jeopardized her freedom to address crowds. Scores of women and children committed civil disobedience to build the Crossroads community and have aroused the conscience of the world. Countless unknown heroes are taking power into their own hands through the important symbolism of flying flags, singing freedom songs, and marching in protest demonstrations.

There is hope here. Humanity survives. In this humanity new forms of creative struggle will emerge, for South Africans and for the rest of the world. In the midst of harsh shadows of death, women and men are determined to create new light, to share that which is already within them. Remember the song from the freedom struggle in the United States: "This little light of mine, I'm going to let it shine." That song was sung most frequently, most creatively, most hopefully in jails, in the face of dogs and rifle butts, under the clouds of tear gas. In the midst of all that it was sung, and the singing has never stopped.

> Only South Africa herself has the power to avert what is rapidly becoming inevitable by demolishing the whole apparatus of apartheid, setting all her peoples free from captivity to the past and offering her immense talents and energy in the service of the development of the whole continent. I am not optimistic, but I have much faith in the providence of God. That alone seems to stand between us and the void.
>
> —Kenneth Kaunda[11]

9

Proposals for Action

... the great South African adventure, that
intense and special dialogue between the people
and the earth which shapes and fashions and
nurtures them, can only begin when the land
is rid of this racial ugliness. This must be
done before there can be any real beginning.
—Peter Abrahams, *A Night of Their Own*[1]

Whomever apartheid touches it damages. The oppressor and
the oppressed are in a relationship which stunts the human
potential of each. The damage from apartheid spreads through
all of southern Africa in widening circles; it profoundly affects economic ties and political antagonisms. Acts of warfare are continuous between SWAPO and South Africa on
the Namibian border. Angola is heavily burdened by frequent South African military forays into its country and by
refugees from Namibia. South Africa carries out sporadic
military raids on its neighbors—Zambia, Zimbabwe, Mozambique, Lesotho, and Botswana. The liberation movements resort to acts of sabotage in the cities and in the countryside. Black or white, South Africans live in fear.

In spite of the anger of the white power structure in South
Africa, the search for justice and peace in South Africa has
become an international concern. What can concerned U.S.
citizens do to contribute to winning this struggle for the

sake of all the people of South Africa? A few suggestions for action are made in this chapter. At a minimum, any relevant action communicates which side of the struggle one selects. Apathy supports apartheid.

Goals and Objectives

The vision for South Africa, or in more pragmatic terms, the goal, is a united, nonracial, just, humane, democratic state. Those who are not South Africans must help make that kind of a state possible. Its internal organization, its political, economic, and social structures, must be the work of South Africans.

Suggested actions for reaching the goal are directed toward two broad objectives: to withdraw support from apartheid and to support South African efforts for change.

Apartheid will flourish in direct proportion to its support. As long as there is foreign acceptance of, cooperation with, and financing of apartheid, it will not disappear. Increased pressures to withdraw such support are essential. Personal involvement in the iniquitous system must be withdrawn for religious and moral reasons. U.S. citizens will primarily be seeking ways to remove the external support for apartheid. However, there are also ways to help South Africans who have withdrawn their support from apartheid.

South African efforts to achieve a just and more egalitarian society can be aided by outside support and encouragement. We, as opponents of apartheid, must be ready to cooperate with and, if possible, participate in the variety of South African efforts for change. We must let all South Africans know of our concern for the quality of life which creative change can bring to all of them.

We must work out in many areas of our life what it means to be committed to the justice of the cause of the oppressed black majority in South Africa.

This will entail entering into the psychic anguish of black South Africans and as Christians regularly holding our sisters and brothers in their suffering, before God in prayer and meditation. It will require repentance on our part, realistic and informed intercession and costly action.

—British Council of Churches in
Whose Rubicon?[2]

Proposals

PUBLIC EDUCATION AND ACTION

These proposals for action will overlap, and the one which overlaps the most is the one for public education, for it can be combined with any form of action. People in the United States are not well informed about South Africa, although the protests and declared emergencies have recently publicized the violence. That alone is not an adequate basis for making sound judgments about the situation in South Africa. It is still not unusual to be asked about the "Union of South Africa," a name dropped twenty-five years ago.

Without basic information about the history of South Africa, the realities of apartheid in daily life and the political structure, and the aspirations and feelings of all the people, one cannot hope to be effective in the promotion of change. Personal experience provides the best educational material. South Africans, returning exchange students, and others with South African experience should be sought as speakers by churches, colleges, service clubs, and other groups. Because of the wide diversity of views on South Africa, it is usually useful to have a panel of two or three speakers. Discussion of the differences of opinion aid the educational process.

Action campaigns all need a large educational component to increase public information and add recruits for further action. There are many proposals to get national, state, or local government action. An informed constituency is the best aid for victory.

Education campaigns are probably most effective when linked to issues of concern to people. Links can be made with labor unions about the export of jobs, as well as with a concern for the international labor movement, workers' rights, and other issues which are universal. Links can be made with women's groups about the double oppression of women, as well as issues of particular concern such as the use of contraceptives considered unsafe for use in the United States but distributed in southern Africa. Links can be made with church groups which can learn about, challenge, and support their sister congregations in South Africa. The strong emphasis on Christianity by apartheid's leaders makes church dialogue on ethical and theological issues particularly important. In other cases, churches in South Africa need support in their opposition to the system.

Public education can lay the foundation for response to crises and become more significant as it provides opportunities for action to those who have learned about South Africa.

ECONOMIC PRESSURES

Economic pressures, along with their pros and cons, were discussed in detail in Chapter 7.

Many actions are possible in the economic arena: the implementation of employment codes, selective withdrawal, boycotts, complete withdrawal, sanctions. Many believe American corporations should leave South Africa. However, whatever position a corporation takes, there are choices to be made which can contribute to the lives of blacks in South Africa. For those corporations which do not withdraw, there are actions that can be put forward at stockholders' meetings which can also serve to educate and inform. Corporations can humanize conditions for some black South Africans by providing training, improved housing, and opportunities for advancement, including training for supervision on a nonracial basis. In a society where full humanity is denied to a majority of the people, actions to affirm that humanity are important.

Corporations can also selectively refuse to participate in the apartheid system. A corporation can challenge the Group Areas Act by providing family housing for workers near the site of employment. The Rietspruit mine, for example, is jointly owned by the Shell Oil Company and the Barlow Rand Company of South Africa. It is unique among South African mines in that it is exempted from the rule that no more than 3 percent of the African employees can be housed with their families at any mine. A corporation could also refuse to take part in the military and security requirements described in Chapter 6. No foreign corporation should operate in South Africa without conscious efforts to improve the lives of blacks and to challenge the apartheid system.

Regardless of workplace reforms or public pronouncements against apartheid, staying in South Africa fosters the status quo. Economic disengagement makes a more significant contribution. To withdraw support from a system is to insist on its change. Withdrawal from the economy of South Africa is an important factor in creating the climate for change. Withdrawal is a direct message. It communicates that those who withdraw will not continue to benefit from or help prolong apartheid. Withdrawal also communicates the strong positive message that the United States looks forward to the time when economic relations with South Africa will be reopened, when it has created a just society for all of its people. Individuals, groups, corporations, and nations should withdraw from present support of the South African economy in order to communicate these clear and direct messages to the people of South Africa.

Selective purchasing by municipalities has become an excellent way to put pressure on U.S. companies doing business in South Africa. More than thirty cities and counties in the United States had some kind of selective purchasing policy by June 1986. Selective purchasing efforts make an excellent opportunity for public education as a city attempts to decide the issue. States can, of course, take similar actions.

A personal boycott of South African products provides an

opportunity to use an educational talking point with other consumers and makes a strong personal statement. The personal boycott helps remove one from complicity in apartheid.

We are now faced with the fact that tomorrow is today. We are confronted with the fierce urgency of now. In this unfolding conundrum of life and history there is such a thing as being too late. Procrastination is still the thief of time. . . . We must move past indecision to action. . . . Now let us begin. Now let us rededicate ourselves to the long and bitter—but beautiful—struggle for a new world. This is the calling of the children of God, and our brothers and sisters wait eagerly for our response. Shall we say the odds are too great? Shall we tell them the struggle is too hard? Or will there be another message, of longing, of hope, of solidarity with their yearnings, of commitment to their cause, whatever the cost? The choice is ours, and though we might prefer it otherwise we must choose in this crucial moment of human history.
—Martin Luther King, Jr.[3]

UNITED STATES GOVERNMENT ACTION

In the first edition of *Challenge and Hope,* published in 1982, it was reported that "the independence of Namibia is a top priority item for the frontline states, the United Nations, the OAU and the Reagan administration's southern African policy . . . Namibia is probably the place where the most useful change could be brought about most quickly in southern Africa" (pp. 122–23).

Five years later that assessment appears to be a bit flawed. The Reagan administration has given little indication that the independence of Namibia has any priority, and there is no expectation for independence to come quickly.

However, to relieve Namibia and its one million people from the oppressive South African rule and a civil war remains a high priority for much of the world. There is agreement, even by the South African government and the U.S. State Department, that independence is to come via implementation of United Nations Resolution 435, which calls for a UN-supervised election.

Cuban troops and technical advisers in Angola are an inadequate excuse for further delay. U.S. citizens must prod Washington to press South Africa for Namibian independence.

The United States has been hesitantly supportive of southern African states (with the exception of Angola), even giving some assistance to Mozambique. Zimbabwe, on South Africa's northern border, is of particular importance in the southern African scene. Zimbabwe's criticisms of U.S. foreign policy must not be allowed to become an excuse to curtail aid. The Southern African Development Coordination Conference (SADCC) has survived its first years with encouraging signs of potential vigor. But SADCC needs help. The U.S. government needs to be encouraged and prodded to find creative ways to strengthen the independence, development, and cooperation of southern African states in their effort to cut dependency on South Africa.

More imaginative ways are needed to apply diplomatic pressure. The United States did recall its ambassador to South Africa at one point and a military attaché at another. Military and commercial attachés should be withdrawn. The United States should sever all military and economic relations with South Africa. Perhaps the ambassador's post should be left vacant until a popularly elected government comes to power. Diplomatic relations should be continued and increased at grassroots levels with labor and cultural affairs. Americans who know the languages should be used to communicate with all sectors of the community.

Other aspects of a U.S. policy designed to press for change in South Africa should include:

—Meaningful ongoing communication with liberation movements in private and in public

—Ceasing the "covert" assistance to UNITA, the guerrilla group attempting to overthrow the government of Angola

—Giving political refugee status to South Africans

—Stepping up educational funding through multinational channels

—Working with the UN on selective sanctions

—Public economic disengagement through corporate withdrawal, sanctions, and a restriction on trade

—Support for congressional attempts at legislation imposing additional sanctions on South Africa, even if certain to be vetoed. Every opportunity should be taken to educate the public on the legislative issues.

The objective is for the U.S. government to give a clear message that this nation insists on the end of apartheid. The Reagan administration has given an unclear message. The powers of this government to move South Africa to change are limited, but that is no excuse for inaction.

In the current debate on U.S. policy toward South Africa, almost all parties—members of Congress, administration officials, corporation executives, religious leaders, political activists—claim to support a nonviolent approach for change in South Africa. Such assertions are sterile and irrelevant if they aren't reinforced by clear action.

INCREASED INTERACTION

Those who advocate divestment, disinvestment, and sanctions are often accused of wanting to sever all links with South Africans. In a speech given in July 1986, President Reagan, in concluding his denunciation of economic withdrawal from South Africa, said: "To make a difference,

Americans—who are a force for decency and progress in the world—must remain involved. We must stay and work, not cut and run."[4]

The choices are not that narrow. Even those persons most negative about South African relationships are supportive of South African liberation movements, political exiles, those who resist conscription, and others who have paid a price to show opposition to apartheid.

Many activists also make a clear distinction between opposing apartheid and supporting the people caught in that system. There is a strong case for increased interaction on a selective basis.

Students, black leaders, and some white leaders who are committed to changing South African society badly need outside support. This may be offered in a number of ways. Students need sponsorship to study abroad. Since education within South Africa is so inadequate for blacks, ways should be sought to help strengthen the pool of leadership through special courses and scholarships.

Well-planned, off-the-record meetings and conferences can involve South Africans in serious discussions of new visions for that country and plans for the transition. Individuals and groups should sponsor those who want and need to come out of South Africa and arrange for South Africans who are abroad to attend special forums in which serious dialogue can occur.

Refugees and exiles need special support. They need direct material aid and political asylum. They also need opportunities for dialogue and planning, including training for future leadership roles—for example, through the liberation organizations and agencies such as the UN Institute for Namibia, operating in Zambia.

For quite different reasons white South Africans need to establish relationships in Zimbabwe and the United States, as well as in many other countries. In Zimbabwe they could experience a nonracial African government striving to meet the needs of all its peoples. They need to see that Zimbabwe is different from what most white South Africans expected. In the United States they could experience the ease with which a society can function with open interracial public accommodations. They could learn about the race problems they will face after apartheid is ended. South Africans have an extremely limited opportunity to know what the rest of the world is like, especially the rest of Africa. There is considerable unreality spawned by their isolation and insulation. Doors need to be opened for fresh experience and new ideas. Communication is critically necessary at many levels.

Access to information is limited in South Africa, so it doesn't happen automatically that the foreign traveler has opportunities for valuable two-way communication. The sensitive traveler is filled with ambiguous feelings because of the inevitable complicity with the apartheid system. The government's authority to grant a visa and to regulate one's daily life in many ways must be accepted. It will become evident to many visitors that that daily life is filled with apartheid regulations ranging from the ridiculous and inconvenient to the immoral and infuriating.

Visits to South Africa by those seeking to make a profit bolster apartheid. This includes visits by entertainers and sports figures or teams who not only violate an internal national boycott but share in South African economic exploitation. The same is true of pleasure trips by tourists. The South African government can often use tourists to support the illusion that South Africa is no different from other countries.

As an example of tourism being used for propaganda purposes, Henry Shank made a visit to South Africa and wrote, in part, to *The Wall Street Journal* (April 7, 1981),

Black settlements in rural and suburban areas compare favorably with housing occupied by blacks in this country. Such places are neat and clean, with gardens, flowers and every evidence of pride in ownership. Certainly there is separatism, but if there are separate hospital entrances, the waiting room I entered was a common one, as was the subsequent attention. Not so different in our country a few years ago, and close up a lot more temperate in practice than we have been led to believe.

Mr. Shanks's letter was quoted at length in *Straight Talk on South Africa* (December 1981), a publication of the South African Ministry of Information. On the front page of the same issue was a picture of the South African Minister of Foreign Affairs chatting with President Reagan in the White House.

On the other hand, visitors can assist change. Visitors are useful if they have a deep moral motivation to support the forces for change, are filled with outrage at a system which denies the humanity of most of its population and which incorporates racism in law as well in the customs. Visitors can share valuable perspectives and information with South Africans whose sources of news and information are restricted. Others may bring expertise or assistance to those working for change. Visitors need to be sure they see and hear a variety of people so that they will be able to share insights and up-to-date news upon their return. They can develop personal human bonds with South Africans, so critical in this intractable and divisive situation.

People who go to South Africa should be willing to witness to their beliefs. They should be willing to confront and challenge the system of apartheid. Searching questions should be asked of those who believe in apartheid, those who passively accept it, and those who challenge it. Love and respect for all people require no less than this kind of honesty.

DIRECT SUPPORT OF SOUTH AFRICANS

Direct financial support to individuals and organizations in South Africa is controversial because the economy is helped by foreign exchange. As in most decision making, there are few "pure" options. Carefully directed contributions to anti-apartheid work outweigh the negative impact of the small increment added to the foreign exchange balance. Such contributions assist in the present and help lay the groundwork for relationships in the post-liberation period.

The South African Council of Churches needs outside support. SACC is a nonracial organization with a majority of black members which has a long record of working against apartheid and speaking with a clear voice. The South African Institute of Race Relations is also nonracial and has continued through the years to supply the world with objective facts about the South African scene. The Black Sash is a courageous group making public protests about apartheid and doing valuable work on the personal legal problems of blacks. The Detainees' Parents Support Committee plays a major role in assisting detainees and their families. The Quaker Service Fund and other denominational groups feed hungry people on a nonpolitical basis at little or no administrative cost to contributors. Black and nonracial labor unions are taking an increasing role in the struggle to build a nonracist society and need assistance.

A second means of direct support to those working for fundamental change in South Africa is the provision of technical and human resources. There are many possibilities, such as legal aid, self-help housing, and vocational training. Responses should be made to particular requests by South Africans. It is not the role of outsiders to determine the priorities or approaches for those in South Africa, including unilateral decisions about the most appropriate aid. Offers should be made in consultation with and in response to requests from South Africans.

Conclusion

The suggestions discussed here may be approached in a variety of ways. Some are more suitable for individuals than for groups. Individuals can, for example, sponsor students and support refugees. Individual actions are transformed and strengthened when joined with others. It is important to involve many people in these actions and the issues behind them in order to change the world climate which allows this unjust system to continue. Some efforts are nongovernmental while others must be focused on U.S. policy and practice. But the racism in U.S. society supports racist and oppressive regimes elsewhere. That problem must continue to be addressed.

There are many ways for people to become involved: accelerated public education campaigns, media campaigns, organized efforts to effect particular pieces of legislation, demonstrations, shareholder activities, nonviolent direct action, and many more options for organizing. All of these should be pursued to change the U.S. impact on South Africa.

A prisoner has a single need: to get out. There may be a multitude of problems after release, but the basic one will be solved with freedom. In the system of apartheid, the South African government is both the jailer and the jailed. That government makes such feeble efforts to free itself that its goals are questionable. The government talks about many changes made and underway, but the international community is unconvinced. Most important of all, black South Africans are not convinced. The world has slowly developed a vision of a world within which the commonality of humanity impels the end to racism, exploitation, and oppression everywhere. White South Africans have a desperate need to share that vision.

South Africa is riding a wild elephant. Is it already too late to dismount? Yes, by the slow process of scrapping bits and pieces of racist laws. No, by releasing Nelson Mandela and other political prisoners; by having meaningful dialogue with ANC and black-selected leaders to negotiate sharing power with the blacks.

10

Liberation Day Plus One

If, at 9 o'clock tomorrow morning, South Africa suddenly had "one man, one vote" the present government would be swept out of office by 9:30. But what would take its place? There is not yet any black South African organization capable of governing successfully. A more likely result would be tribal warfare, butchery, bloodshed and devastation. In too many African nations, "one man, one vote" has been a one-way ticket to tyranny.
—Raymond Price, columnist and former speech writer for President Richard Nixon[1]

The Raymond Price idea is widely held by white South Africans and continually propagated by the South African government. At the opening of the 1986 session of Parliament in Cape Town, P. W. Botha, State President, once again told his listeners that if the present Republic should fall it would be replaced by "a one-party dictatorship." The irony of the fact that South Africa has been under the repressive dictatorship of a single party with no viable opposition in Parliament since the Nationalists won power in 1948 seems to escape not only P. W. Botha but much of the general public in the United States.

Speakers on South Africa in this country, activists in the divestment movement, and other advocates of ending domination by whites in South Africa face numerous questions which imply that the post-liberation period may be much worse than the present. Won't white racism be traded for black racism? Won't tribalism tear the country apart? Won't the Communists take over? How about corruption? How about crime and violence? Look at the multiple coups elsewhere in Africa. Look at Uganda. Look at the economy of Mozambique, Zambia, Tanzania, or almost anywhere else in Africa.

These questions reflect valid concerns, both for the prospects of change and for the prospects for the future of South Africa. Many of these questions have been dealt with in preceding chapters. Often, however, such questions are asked to deflect change, express fears, and buttress the status quo or are, in part, a reflection of racism or paternalism. Without knowing the timing, nature, or context of the transfer of power, there can be no guaranteed answers to questions about the transition, but it can be predicted with certainty that the nature and severity of the problems of transition will be directly related to the nature and severity of the circumstances surrounding the transfer of power.

Many Americans look at Africa through glasses tinted with racism and paternalism. The stereotypes of "primitive" Africans, well-meaning and in need of direction from others, is reinforced in the U.S. culture in ways far more effective than the self-serving propaganda distributed by the South African government.

Hollywood's contribution to the African stereotype is enormous, most recently in the award-winning movie *Out of Africa*. Typical of the distortions which bolster stereotypes was the incident of African children clustered together to hear the cuckoo clock and then frightened away when the cuckoo emerged. The audience always laughs; they have superior knowledge about cuckoo clocks. But in the book the children do not run away. They gather about the clock with anticipation as it is about to strike noon and hear it with great amusement.

The same reaction may be seen at the British Museum, which has a noted collection of clocks, where people, mostly white Western adults, move from one clock to another and anticipate the variety of striking mechanisms which mark the hour. The marking of the hour is heard and watched with great amusement.

> They left their flocks on the lawn and came in noiselessly on their bare feet; the bigger ones were about ten years and the youngest two years. They behaved very well, and kept up a sort of self-made ceremonial for their visits, which came to this: that they could move freely in the house so long as they did not touch anything, nor sit down, nor speak unless spoken to. As the cuckoo rushed out on them, a great movement of ecstasy and suppressed laughter ran through the group.
> —Isak Dinesen, *Out of Africa*[2]

Liberation Has Problems

As Conor Cruise O'Brien wrote: "Even after apartheid and all its elaborate mutations have been thrown to rust on the scrap heap of history, South Africa will still have enormous problems. . . . It may be nearly as hard for a black government to control Soweto as it is for a white government."[3]

O'Brien makes only passing reference to these difficulties, with no attempt either to identify them or to suggest solutions. If the present South African government has any ideas or plans about the post-liberation period, they are not disclosing them, and it is unlikely that they are willing or able to think within that context. Liberation movements have often eschewed developing detailed plans for the period after liberation as a premature diversion of resources needed to obtain liberation. The post-liberation government, probably made up of a coalition not accustomed to working together closely, will inherit an infrastructure which cannot be foreseen in much detail and will go to work without a plan of operation. This fact alone assures a rough period of transition.

There will be the usual competition, as in every part of the world, for power. This competition will be within the successful coalition, as well as between the coalition and those who unsuccessfully contest it. Unfortunately, the internal struggle for power will attract external participants. As white-ruled South Africa has destabilized its neighbors, it may be subject to destabilization after liberation. Countries from either the right or the left or both may put economic, military, or other pressures on the new government.

Another built-in problem of transition from racist minority rule to "people power" will be the expectations of the people. Many will expect instant results from the radical change. In Zimbabwe, workers expecting huge pay increases staged numerous strikes immediately after independence. The new government, not the employers, had to settle this problem. Fortunately, this was worked through quickly and successfully in Zimbabwe. Problems ranging from corruption to lower productivity to political disaffection may result from overly optimistic expectations. Sometimes expectations are reasonable, but expected impossibly soon; it will take time to provide adequate educational and medical services, better housing, and land.

There Are Special Problems

In addition to problems normal to countries which have had to struggle to end minority rule, South Africa is cursed with special problems of its own created by apartheid. The superficial view is of a black/white problem, but apartheid has taken "apartness" much deeper than that. Not only is everyone classified by race, with subdivisions, but within the segregated townships people are even assigned housing in certain sections by a determination of tribal classification. By manipulating ethnic classification, the South African government has convinced itself that South Africa is a complex of minorities. The whites are not only just one of the minorities, they are one of the largest by government calculation.

As the designers and beneficiaries of apartheid, whites will obviously create difficulties. White commando groups are already in operation; they have assassinated black leaders, and a few participants have been prosecuted by the present government. Although the present white commando units have Afrikaans names, it should be remembered that there are also right-wing English-speaking South Africans who may join such units.

White intransigence is not limited to commandos. Top government circles declare openly that an end-of-the-line solution for whites is a white "homeland," a laager enclosing a considerable part of South Africa. An official South African government publication reported in a lead article: "In short: no possibility exists that a Black government coming to power by pressure from outside, will ever govern a united South Africa. This simple truth should be considered more often by advocates of sanctions and disinvestment."[4]

The new government may call itself capitalist, African socialist, Marxist, or something else. Whatever it calls itself, it will face tremendous problems in restructuring the economy. The widespread poverty, the maldistribution of wealth, and the history of racially based economic exploitation will face any new government with the immediate need for economic change. This raises difficult technical problems of economics, and even more difficult political and social problems, to meet human needs and expectations while keeping the wealth-producing infrastructure of South Africa in full operation.

The government has cut our country into enclaves. This enclave is for those Zulu Kaffirs, that

> enclave is for those Xhosa Kaffirs, that enclave is
> for those Pedi Kaffirs—that is what the so-called
> homeland puppets have accepted. Pretoria pulls the
> strings and directs them as to what they should
> think, and uses them to oppress their people. These
> people suck the dummies from their masters in
> Pretoria, where their feeding bottle is sterilized and
> refilled. They have become their master's own
> voice.   —Winnie Mandela[5]

The homelands represent another prospect for intransigence. The final report of the constitutional committee stated
that it is inconceivable that the process of homeland "independence" could be checked or reversed peacefully.
KwaNdebele is scheduled to receive "independence." If this
happens, there will be five "independent" homelands and
five homelands which have stated that they don't wish "independence." Irrespective of the differences in political status, all of the homelands have a top leader and a sizable
cadre of other leaders who have more status, power, and
wealth than they are apt to have within the post-liberation
period. Many of those working for liberation write off the
current crop of homeland leaders as a collection of stooges
who are cooperating in the apartheid system.

Chief Mangosuthu Gatsha Buthelezi and his followers
represent a particular problem created by apartheid, almost
certain to be difficult to assimilate into the post-liberation
transition. Buthelezi heads the Zulu tribe, one of the largest;
the KwaZulu homeland, for which he rejects "independence"; and Inkatha, a large, mostly Zulu, political and cultural movement. Buthelezi is an astute politician, difficult to
predict. He claims to reject the homeland policy "vehe-
mently," yet he heads a homeland. He is supposed to be
close to State President Botha, yet he recently declared of

Botha: "This man has got his head so deeply buried in the sand that you will have to recognize him by the shape of his toes."[6]

Buthelezi is a publicly outspoken foe of apartheid and violence who does not carry out nonviolent resistance to apartheid and whose followers harass the United Democratic Front and ravage an Indian community in Durban without reproof from him. He is an implacable foe of ANC who has stated that he might participate in a "marriage of convenience" with ANC and PAC.[7] He is lauded by the white power structure of South Africa; for example, he received the Pretoria Press Club's Newsmaker of the Year award on March 20, 1986. He is a newsmaker and a likely problem maker in the post-liberation period, either on the inside or on the outside of the new power structure.

White intransigence, homelands, restructuring of the economy, and Chief Buthelezi represent special problems growing out of apartheid. The underlying problem will be racism, ingrained in law, fundamental to the only culture most of the population has known.

And I am waiting
for a way to be devised
to destroy all nationalism
without killing anybody
  . . .
and I am perpetually waiting
for the fleeing lovers on the Grecian Urn
to catch each other at last
and embrace
and I am awaiting
perpetually and forever
a renaissance of wonder
    —from Lawrence Ferlinghetti, "I Am Waiting"[8]

In the face of overwhelming odds against a peaceful transition, there are those who advocate "go slowly," saying "change must come by evolution." There are also those who say that the limited stability of the present is better than the expected lack of stability in the "one person, one vote" society to come.

What about Freedom?

Blacks are incensed by the call to go slowly, a call they have heard for decades. Who has the right to suggest to black South Africans that the known evils of today are better than the promises of tomorrow?

What about freedom? What about self-determination? The struggle is, in part, about the right of people to make their own mistakes about their own lives. These are values the United States holds high. The future of South Africa will be built on centuries of mistakes, and there is still a close relationship between sowing and reaping. No one should be surprised if it takes years, perhaps decades, to build an effective, humane, stable government for and by the people— all of the people, or even the majority of the people.

The immediate reaction to liberation will be one of joy and relief for most of the population of South Africa. The energy released by the laying down of the old struggle and the enthusiasm for a new order will be an immediate asset for building the new society.

South Africa also has special strengths for the transition. There are far more South African black college graduates than any other African country had at the time of independence. South Africa is rich in natural resources to help finance the new society. The struggle for majority rule has involved most of the world, and there will be international resources available to help the new government. The international individual and organizational energies and resources which are going into movements such as the divestment campaign probably could be diverted to aid South Africa in transition. Behind the furor in and over South Africa at the present time there are many almost unnoticed economic and social institutions organized and operated by blacks. These institutions are already part of the new society. There are South Africans of all races who have demonstrated their willingness to work for a new peaceful society. The growing role of the church—black, white, and racially integrated—has been discussed in Chapter 4. The church as an institution and church leaders are valuable resources for the transition. The positive forces for change are many.

Liberation day plus one will inevitably be difficult, perhaps in some ways as difficult as the pre-liberation years. One cannot escape one's time. The post-liberation time will need understanding of the difficulties of the day, creativity, and recognition of the worth of all participants. The challenge of liberation will be great, but in the struggle to build a new society, people will reach out with hope.

Chronology

1652	First settlement at the Cape of Good Hope by Europeans (Dutch East India Company); Khoikhoi and San already in area
1657	Dutch East India Company frees a few employees to create the nucleus of settlers
1658	First substantial importation of slaves
1659–60	First Khoikhoi-Dutch war
1673–77	Second Khoikhoi-Dutch war
1688	Arrival of 200 French Huguenot settlers
1700	European population reaches 1,000
1779–81	First frontier war with Xhosa
1793	Second frontier war
1795	First British occupation of the Cape
1799	Third frontier war
1800	European population reaches 20,000
1803	Cape restored temporarily to Dutch rule
1806	Second British occupation
1807	Abolition of the slave trade in British Empire
1814	British acquire permanent sovereignty over the Cape
1820	Arrival of 5,000 British immigrants

1828	British make English the official language of South Africa
1829	University of Cape Town started
1834–35	Major war with Xhosa on the eastern frontier; English and Dutch involved
1836–38	The Great Trek
1838	Trekking Boers defeat Zulu at the Battle of Blood River Founding of the Boer Republic in Natal Completion of slave emancipation in Cape Colony
1843	British annexation of Natal
1848	British government proclaims its sovereignty between the Orange and Vaal rivers
1852	British recognize the independence of the Boers in the Transvaal
1854	British grant independence to the Orange Free State Cape Colony granted representative government; establishment of nonracial franchise
1858	Founding of the South African Republic by the Boers in the Transvaal
1860	Indian indentured laborers introduced into Natal by British
1867	Discovery of diamonds
1872	Cape Colony granted responsible cabinet government
1877	Annexation of the Transvaal by the British
1879	British-Zulu war
1880	First Anglo-Boer war
1881	Transvaal Republic regains its independence
1884	Europeans begin exploitation of gold field in Transvaal South West Africa becomes German Protectorate
1893	Natal granted responsible government
1894	Mahatma Gandhi arrives in South Africa Natal Indian Congress formed

1895	The Jameson raid (abortive attempt by pro-British to overthrow the Transvaal government)
1899	Outbreak of the second Anglo-Boer war
1902	End of Anglo-Boer war (called Second War of Freedom by Afrikaners)
1905	South African Native Affairs Commission advocates territorial segregation of whites and Africans
1906	Gandhi coins word *Satyagraha* ("force which is born of truth and love") Zulu rebellion in Natal
1907	Cape Colony School Board Act restricts access of non-whites to public education Asiatic Registration Act passed by Transvaal Gandhi-led resistance campaign begins Attainment of Responsible Government by the Transvaal and the Orange Free State in preparation for union
1909	South African Native Convention meets, asks extension of Cape franchise and end of color bar
1910	Establishment of the Union of South Africa
1911	Mine and Works Act of Union Parliament sanctions an industrial color bar Strikes by Africans made a crime
1912	African National Congress founded
1913	Natives Land Act prohibits Africans from buying land outside of reserves
1915	Mahatma Gandhi leads march of over 2,000 Indians into the Transvaal, courting arrest
1918	Broederbond founded
1919	ANC anti-pass campaign, 700 arrests in Johannesburg 400 dockworkers strike in Cape Town
1920	South West Africa mandated to South Africa by the League of Nations
1926	Colour Bar Act secures a monopoly on skilled jobs for white mine workers South African Indian Congress formed

1930	White women enfranchised Three blacks killed by police at pass-burning demonstration
1931	Statute of Westminster confirms dominion status to South Africa
1932	African women organize passive resistance against curfew regulations in the Transvaal
1934	Founding of Purified National Party by Afrikaner opponents of Hertzog's coalition.
1936	Africans removed from the common voters' roll in Cape Province
1943	Alexandra bus boycott African Mineworkers Union strike involving 73,557 workers; 9 killed by police
1944	600 Indians jailed in Natal passive resistance against segregation Congress Youth League formed
1945	Dr. A. B. Zuma publishes *African Claims,* applying Atlantic Charter ideas to South Africa Black Urban Areas Consolidation Act creates system of black townships
1946	African mine workers' strike broken by police Nearly 2,000 Indians (and a few whites, including Rev. Michael Scott) jailed in Natal for nonviolent resistance to anti-Indian legislation UN General Assembly denies South Africa's request to annex South West Africa
1948	National Party victory over the United Party in parliamentary elections
1949	Prohibition of Mixed Marriages Act Population Registration Act ANC Youth League calls for civil disobedience and noncooperation against pass law and apartheid
1950	Group Areas Act Police fire on mass labor strike in the Transvaal; 18 blacks killed

Suppression of Communism Act makes Communist Party unlawful

1951   Bantu Authorities Act establishes a new system of government for African reserves

1952   ANC and Indian Congress deliberately break segregation laws in the Defiance Campaign Against Unjust Laws 8,000 arrested nationwide, 14 killed by police, 35 wounded

1953   Reservation of Separate Amenities Act
Bantu Education Act
Federation of Rhodesia and Nyasaland formed

1954   World Council of Churches makes strong statement against racism without dissent

1955   10,000 children stay out of school in Bantu Education Act protest
Freedom Charter adopted

1956   Thousands of African women protest pass laws; 3 killed by police
Coloureds removed from common voters' roll in Cape Province
Treason trial of 156 persons

1959   Pan Africanist Congress formed by Robert Sobukwe

1960   A. J. Luthuli wins Nobel Peace Prize
SWAPO organized
Sharpeville Massacre
Cottesloe ecumenical consultation
PAC and ANC banned

1961   South Africa becomes a republic and severs ties with the British Commonwealth
ANC organizes Umkonto We Sizwe (Spear of the Nation)

1962   "Sabotage Act" greatly broadens South African government's repressive powers

1963   Organization of African Unity founded
UN passes voluntary arms embargo against South Africa
Nelson Mandela, Walter Sisulu, et al. sentenced to life

in prison under the Suppression of Communism Act
Federation of Rhodesia and Nyasaland disbanded
African women required to carry reference books,
"passes"

1964   Malawi becomes independent
Zambia becomes independent

1965   Southern Rhodesia Unilateral Declaration of Independence

1966   Herman Toivo ja Toivo, SWAPO founder, sentenced
to twenty years in prison
Botswana becomes independent
Lesotho becomes independent
UN terminates South African mandate over Namibia

1968   Creation of Coloured Persons' Representative Council
(terminated 1980)
Swaziland becomes independent
South Africa bans multiracial membership in political
parties and Liberal Party disbands

1969   Steve Biko elected first President of South African Students' Organization (SASO)

1970   UN Security Council Resolution 283 calls on all countries to end economic involvement of their nationals in
Namibia
First World Council of Churches grant for humanitarian needs of southern African liberation movements

1971   African workers strike in Namibia and win minor
concessions
World Council of Churches withdraws invested funds
from corporations operating in South Africa
World Court holds South African administration of
Namibia terminated

1972   Black dockworkers strike in Durban and win pay increase

1973   First British Council of Churches study on investment
in South Africa
UN General Assembly declares SWAPO to be "sole
authentic representative of the people of Namibia"

70,000 strike in Durban, Cape Town, and Hammersdale

1975   Mozambique becomes independent
Angola becomes independent

1976   Soweto uprising; protests spread across the country, over 1,000 killed
Transkei declared independent by South Africa

1977   Steve Biko killed while in police custody
UN approves mandatory arms embargo against South Africa
17 Black Consciousness organizations and the Christian Institute declared unlawful
Bophuthatswana declared independent by South Africa

1978   Azanian African People's Organization (AZAPO), a Black Consciousness group, organized
UN Security Council endorses Resolution 435 as Namibian settlement plan

1979   British Council of Churches calls for economic disengagement from South Africa and an international oil boycott
Bantu Education Act replaced by Education and Training Act, No. 90
Venda declared independent by South Africa

1980   Zimbabwe becomes independent

1981   Geneva conference on Namibia fails to reach agreement
National Party wins new election but with loss of votes to both liberals and conservatives
Ciskei declared independent by South Africa

1982   UN General Assembly proclaims 1982 as the International Year of Mobilization for Sanctions against South Africa
National Party in South Africa splits, with formation of right-wing Conservative Party of South Africa

1983   United Democratic Front (UDF) organized

1984   Bishop Desmond Tutu awarded Nobel Peace Prize

Tricameral Parliament inaugurated and protests spread across South Africa

1985   Congress of South African Trade Unions (COSATU) formed
State President Botha declares state of emergency over much of South Africa (July 21)
South Africa suspends debt payments

1986   State of emergency lifted (March 7)
South Africa makes military strikes against Zimbabwe, Zambia, and Botswana on the same day (May 19)
Pass laws repealed
Nationwide state of emergency declared and thousands detained (June 12)
U.S. Congress passes broad South African sanctions bill over the President's veto
Samora Machel, President of Mozambique, killed in plane crash

Notes

CHAPTER 1

1. British Council of Churches, *Political Change in South Africa: Britain's Responsibility* (London, 1979), p. 2.

2. Precise estimates vary depending on source and timing. For example, recent official South African government statistics indicate that 13.7 percent of the land is now allocated to Africans as a result of land transfers to the so-called independent states. At the same time, however, Africans have been relocated from lands, so precise allocations are in flux. This point is made in such detail to illustrate a continuing problem with all figures in this book. In any situation where political opinions are sharply divided, the choice of figures reflects political biases. In this book, the range of available figures is considered and the most credible are used.

3. South African Institute of Race Relations, *Race Relations Survey 1984* (Johannesburg), p. 84.

4. *Ibid.*, p. 735.

5. *Ibid.*, p. 186.

6. *Ibid.*, p. 185.

7. *The Star* (Johannesburg), June 29, 1984, as quoted in *South African Digest*, July 6, 1984.

8. South African Institute of Race Relations, *Survey of Race Relations in South Africa 1983* (Johannesburg), p. 302.

9. South African Institute of Race Relations, *Race Relations Survey 1984*, p. 468.

10. *Ibid.*, p. 437.

11. South African Institute of Race Relations, *Survey of Race Relations in South Africa 1983*, p. 302.

12. *Ibid.*, p. 303.

13. New York *Times*, August 11, 1981.

14. United Nations Economic Commission for Africa, *Women and Apartheid in South Africa and Namibia* (Addis Ababa, 1984), p. 1.

15. South African Institute of Race Relations, *Race Relations Survey 1984*, p. 241.

16. *Ibid.*, p. 650.

17. Kenneth Kaunda, *The Riddle of Violence* (San Francisco: Harper & Row, 1980), pp. 174–77.

18. *South African Digest* (Pretoria), reprinted as the lead essay, February 24, 1984.

19. Washington *Post*, February 19, 1982.

20. Ken Owens, in *CSIS Africa Notes*, January 31, 1986.

21. Philadelphia *Inquirer*, May 7, 1986.

22. Donald Woods, *Asking for Trouble* (New York: Atheneum, 1981), p. 9.

23. Dennis Brutus, *A Simple Lust* (New York: Hill and Wang, 1973), p. 4.

CHAPTER 2

1. Based on a map in *White Supremacy: A Comparative Study in American and South African History*, George M. Fredrickson (New York: Oxford University Press, 1971).

2. Vincent Crapanzano, *Waiting: The Whites of South Africa* (New York: Random House, 1985), p. 103.

CHAPTER 3

1. Albert Luthuli, *Let My People Go: The Autobiography of a Great African Leader* (Johannesburg: Collins, 1962), p. 130.

2. Monica Wilson and Leonard Thompson, eds., *The Oxford History of South Africa*, Vol. I (New York and Oxford: Oxford University Press, 1969).

3. Julius Lewin, *Politics and Law in South Africa* (London: Merlin Press, 1963), pp. 47–48; reprinted from *The Political Quarterly* (London), 1953.

4. The Freedom Charter was adopted at a "Congress of the People" in Kliptown, South Africa, in June 1955. The meeting was called by the African National Congress, the South African Indian Congress, the South African Coloured People's Organization, and the Congress of Democrats.

5. South African Institute of Race Relations, *Survey of Race Relations in South Africa 1980* (Johannesburg), p. 246.

CHAPTER 4

1. South African Institute of Race Relations, *Survey of Race Relations in South Africa 1983* (Johannesburg), p. 568.

2. Catholic Institute for International Relations, *South Africa in the 1980s: State of Emergency* (3rd ed.; London, 1986), p. 30.

3. South African Institute of Race Relations, *Race Relations Survey 1984* (Johannesburg), p. 858.

4. *Mission to South Africa: The Commonwealth Report* (Advance copy; London, 1986), paragraph 121, p. 21.

5. New York *Times,* June 22, 1986.

6. Taped interview of Allan Boesak in South Africa with British Council of Churches delegation, September 1985.

7. *Non-Violence News,* First Quarter, 1986. South African Council of Churches Justice and Reconciliation Division, Johannesburg, p. 1.

8. *South African Digest* (Pretoria), June 20, 1986.

9. *Manchester Guardian Weekly,* June 8, 1986.

10. Conor Cruise O'Brien, "What Can Become of South Africa?," *The Atlantic Monthly,* March 1986, p. 67.

CHAPTER 5

1. Based on a map in *Backgrounder,* September 1981, South African Department of Foreign Affairs and Information, Pretoria.

2. Interview with the Afrikaans newspaper *Beeld* (Johannesburg), April 30, 1986; reprinted in *South African Digest,* May 9, 1986, p. 402.

3. Sanford Ungar and Peter Vale, "South Africa: Why Constructive Engagement Failed," *Foreign Affairs,* Winter 1985–86, p. 235.

4. Bishop Desmond Tutu, taped message to the Trans Africa Forum, February 1982, quoted in *Hope and Suffering* (Grand Rapids, Mich.: Eerdmans, 1984), p. 117.

5. *The Economist* (London), editorial, September 5, 1981.

CHAPTER 6

1. Martin Minogue and Judith Molloy, eds., *African Aims and Attitudes: Selected Documents* (London: Cambridge University Press, 1974).

2. *Mission to South Africa: The Commonwealth Report* (Advance copy; London, 1986), paragraph 335, p. 63.

3. *Ibid.*

4. *South African Digest* (Pretoria), June 13, 1986.

5. *Mission to South Africa: The Commonwealth Report,* paragraph 339, pp. 64–65.

6. The major South African parastatals are: ARMSCOR, for the development, production, procurement, and sale of military armaments; ISCOR, iron and steel production; ESCOM, the production of electricity, including nuclear power; SAR&H, railway and harbor operations; SENTRACHEM, chemical production; SASOL, coal, oil, and gas corporation; oil from coal production.

7. Robert I. Rotberg, *Suffer the Future: Policy Choices in Southern Africa* (Cambridge: Harvard University Press, 1980), pp. 130–31.

8. South African Department of Foreign Affairs, *A Vision of New Structures* (Pretoria, 1985).

9. South African Department of Foreign Affairs, *Reform in South Africa* (Pretoria, 1985).

CHAPTER 7

1. John Vorster in a 1972 statement when he was the Prime Minister of South Africa. Quoted in the New York *Times,* June 15, 1986.

2. R. F. Botha, South African Minister of Foreign Affairs, in the House of Assembly, as reported in *South African Digest* (Pretoria), May 9, 1986.

3. Bishop Desmond Tutu, as reported in *South African Digest,* April 11, 1986.

4. *The Times* (London), April 7, 1986.

5. Dr. C. F. Beyers Naudé, General Secretary of the South African Council of Churches, speaking in London, November 25, 1985.

6. Investor Responsibility Research Center, Washington, D.C.

7. Philadelphia *Inquirer,* April 16, 1986.

8. Windhoek *Advertiser,* May 13, 1986.

9. *South African Digest,* March 21, 1986.

10. *Ibid.,* March 28, 1986.

11. Central Statistical Services, Pretoria.

12. U.S. Department of State, "The U.S. Approach to South Africa," Current Policy No. 854, July 1986, p. 2.

13. Albert Luthuli, *Let My People Go: The Autobiography of a Great African Leader* (Johannesburg: Collins, 1962).

14. *Africa News,* June 2, 1986, pp. 1–5.

15. Flora Lewis, New York *Times,* June 15, 1986, Op-Ed page.

16. In a lecture at the University of the Witwatersrand, Johannesburg, September 4, 1980.

17. New York *Times,* July 27, 1986.

18. *The Observer* (London), editorial comment, May 25, 1986.

19. *The Journal of John Woolman and A Plea for the Poor,* John Greenleaf Whittier Edition Text (New York: Corinth Books, 1961), p. 241.

20. *Economic Notes,* Labor Research Association, New York, July–August 1985, p. 3.

21. South African Institute of Race Relations, *Race Relations Survey 1984* (Johannesburg), p. 318.

CHAPTER 8

1. Kenneth Kaunda, *The Riddle of Violence* (San Francisco: Harper & Row, 1980), p. 67.

2. Dr. Jan S. Marais, *South Africa: Target or Opportunity* (Cape Town: Makew Miller, 1981), pp. 7–8.

3. From resolution approved at Christian Institute meeting of the Board of Directors in Pietermaritzburg, September 20, 1976.

4. Philip S. Foner, ed., *The Life and Writings of Frederick Douglass* (New York: International Publishers, 1950), Vol. II, p. 437.

5. The Kairos Document, *Challenge to the Church: A Theological Comment on the Political Crisis in South Africa* (Braamfontein: Kairos Theologians, 1985), p. 9.

6. Margaret Hope Bacon, compiler, *Lucretia Mott Speaking* (Wallingford, Pa.: Pendle Hill Publications, 1980), Pendle Hill Pamphlet No. 234, pp. 18, 22.

7. Gwendolen M. Carter, *Which Way Is South Africa Going?* (Bloomington: Indiana University Press, 1980), p. 12.

8. Kaunda, *op. cit.,* p. 170.

9. "Between January and March 1973, African workers seeking higher wages struck approximately 150 Natal firms one after another without any apparent overall organization or even obvious leaders" (Carter, *op. cit.,* p. 93). By 1986 the labor unions had begun to work with and have strikes led by their recognized leaders.

10. The Kairos Document, pp. 11–12.

11. Kaunda, *op. cit.,* p. 178.

CHAPTER 9

1. Peter Abrahams, *A Night of Their Own* (New York: Alfred A. Knopf, 1965), p. 220.

2. British Council of Churches, *Whose Rubicon?,* report of a visit to South Africa by representatives of the British churches (London, 1986), p. 53.

3. A compilation of Martin Luther King's statements; the beginning and the major portion are from *Where Do We Go from Here: Chaos or Community?* (New York: Bantam, 1968), p. 222.

4. Address by President Ronald Reagan to the World Affairs Council and Foreign Policy Association, Washington, D.C., July 22, 1986; printed in U.S. Department of State, Bureau of Public Affairs, Current Policy No. 853, p. 3.

CHAPTER 10

1. Raymond Price, Philadelphia *Inquirer,* March 10, 1986, Op-Ed page.

2. Isak Dinesen, *Out of Africa* (New York: Random House, Modern Library, 1952), p. 47.

3. Conor Cruise O'Brien, "What Can Become of South Africa?," *The Atlantic Monthly,* March 1986, pp. 41–68.

4. *South African Digest* (Pretoria), April 4, 1986; reprinted from the Afrikaans newspaper *Beeld* (Johannesburg), March 12, 1986.

5. Winnie Mandela, *Part of My Soul Went with Him* (New York: Norton, 1985), p. 122.

6. Philadelphia *Inquirer,* April 9, 1986.

7. South African Institute of Race Relations, *Survey of Race Relations in South Africa 1983* (Johannesburg), p. 346.

8. Lawrence Ferlinghetti, *A Coney Island of the Mind* (New York: New Directions, 1955), p. 49.

Appendix

Abbreviations

AFSC	American Friends Service Committee
ANC	African National Congress
ARMSCOR	Armaments Development and Productions Company
AWB	Afrikaner Weerstandsbeweging
AZAPO	Azanian African People's Organization
BCC	British Council of Churches
BCM	Black Consciousness Movement
BCP	Black Community Programs
BPC	Black People's Convention
COSAS	Council of South African Students
COSATU	Congress of South African Trade Unions
CUSA	Council of Unions of South Africa
DRC	Dutch Reformed Church
DTA	Democratic Turnhalle Alliance
EEC	European Economic Community
ESCOM	Electricity Supply Commission
FOSATU	Federation of South African Trade Unions
FRELIMO	Front for the Liberation of Mozambique
HNP	Herstigte Nasionale Party
ISCOR	South African Iron and Steel Industrial Corporation
LLA	Lesotho Liberation Army
MNR	Mozambique National Resistance Movement
MPC	Multi-Party Conference (Namibia)

MPLA	Popular Movement for the Liberation of Angola
NECC	National Education Crisis Committee
NIS	National Intelligence Service (South Africa)
NUM	National Union of Mineworkers
NUSAS	National Union of South African Students
OAU	Organization of African Unity
PAC	Pan Africanist Congress
PFP	Progressive Federal Party
QPS	Quaker Peace and Service (London)
SAA	South African Airways
SABC	South African Broadcasting Corporation
SADCC	Southern African Development Coordination Conference
SADF	South African Defence Force
SAIRR	South African Institute of Race Relations
SAR&H	South African Railways and Harbors
SASM	South African Student Movement
SASO	South African Students' Organization
SASOL	South African Coal, Oil, and Gas Corporation
SOWETO	South West Townships
SWAPO	South West African People's Organization
SWATF	South West African Territorial Force
TBVC	Transkei, Bophuthatswana, Venda, Ciskei
UDF	United Democratic Front
UDI	Unilateral Declaration of Independence (Southern Rhodesia)
UNITA	National Union for the Total Independence of Angola
UWUSA	United Workers Union of South Africa
WCC	World Council of Churches
ZANU-PF	Zimbabwe National Union (Patriotic Front)
ZAPU	Zimbabwe African People's Union

Glossary

African National Congress (ANC): South African liberation movement. Founded in 1912.

Africans: Used in this book for black ethnic groups originating in Africa. Most Afrikaners consider themselves to be white Africans.

Afrikaans: Language developed from seventeenth-century Dutch by Afrikaners. Spoken only in South Africa.

Afrikaner Resistance Movement (Afrikaner Weerstandsbeweging): One of a number of pro-apartheid groups.

Afrikaners: White persons of Dutch-Huguenot ancestry whose first language is Afrikaans and who first immigrated to South Africa in the seventeenth century.

Amandla Ngawethu!: Zulu for "Power is ours!"

Angola: Former Portuguese territory. Independent in 1975.

Apartheid: The South African economic, political, and social system based on race; "separateness."

ARMSCOR: South African parastatal corporation which produces and procures weapons.

Azania: Name used by PAC and Black Consciousness organizations for South Africa. ANC, and those sympathetic to ANC, do not use this name.

Azanian African People's Organization (AZAPO): Black Consciousness group.

Bantu: Word used in South Africa as synonymous with "African." Disliked by blacks; properly refers to a linguistic group.

Bantu Education Act: Law on African education from 1953 to 1979. Designed to educate Africans for their "proper place."

Bantustan: Early name for areas now called homelands.

Biko, Steve: First President of South African Students' Organization, a leader of Black Consciousness Movement. Died while in police custody, 1977.

Black Consciousness Movement: South African black power movement; crosses African political and ethnic lines.

Blacks: Usually means Africans, Indians, and coloured. Sometimes, particularly in South Africa, means only Africans.

Black Sash: Organization of women, predominantly white, who wear black sashes in frequent demonstrations against apartheid.

Boers: First designation of group now called Afrikaners. Literally, in Dutch, "farmers."

Boesak, Dr. Allan: President of the World Alliance of Reformed Churches.*

Bophuthatswana: South African homeland. "Independent" 1977.

Botha, P. W.: State President of South Africa.*

Botha, R. F.: ("Pik"): Minister of Foreign Affairs for South Africa.*

Botswana: Former British Protectorate called Bechuanaland. Independent 1966.

Broederbond: Secret society of Afrikaner leaders, a behind-the-scenes power center.

Brutus, Dennis: Black South African poet, a political exile in the United States.

Buthelezi, Mangosuthu Gatsha: Zulu leader, Chief Minister of KwaZulu and head of Inkatha.*

Cape Province: One of the four provinces of South Africa.

Christian Institute: Interracial, ecumenical organization founded by Rev. Beyers Naudé to work against apartheid. Banned October 1977.

Ciskei: South African homeland. "Independent" 1981.

Coloureds: Persons of mixed-race ancestry. The majority have Afrikaans as a first language.

Congress Youth League: Youth section of ANC, founded 1943.

---

*Office held at time of publication.

Conservative Party of South Africa: New party formed in 1982 in a right-wing split from National Party.

Contact Group: United States, United Kingdom, France, Canada, West Germany. Group working on resolution of issues between SWAPO and South Africa for independence of Namibia.

Cottesloe: Ecumenical South African consultation on racism. Called by World Council of Churches subsequent to Sharpeville, 1960. (Named after place of meeting.)

Crocker, Chester: U.S. Assistant Secretary of State for African Affairs.*

Crossroads: African squatter community outside of Cape Town.

Democratic Turnhalle Alliance: Coalition of Namibian political parties formerly in office under South African settlement attempt. Dominated by whites.

Dos Santos, José Eduardo: President of Angola.*

Education and Training Act, No. 90: Replacement for Bantu Education Act.

Eglin, Colin: Leader of Progressive Federal Party.*

Freedom Charter: Adopted by the Congress of the People (a coalition of ANC and other organizations) in 1955 stating African aspirations for a nonracial, egalitarian state for South Africa.

Front for the Liberation of Mozambique (FRELIMO): Ruling party in Mozambique.

Frontline states: Originally included states bordering on Zimbabwe except South Africa, plus Angola and Tanzania. Now loosely applied to all states of southern Africa, plus Tanzania, as frontline to South Africa.

Group Areas Act: South African law which segregates areas by race.

---

*Office held at time of publication.

Herstigte Nasionale Party: Right-wing, pro-apartheid political party.

Homelands: South African government designation for rural areas reserved for Africans according to ethnic groups.

Identity card: Must be carried by all South Africans.

Impi: Group of Zulu males of paramilitary nature.

Influx control: System for keeping unemployed Africans out of "white" cities.

Inkatha: Cultural, social, and political organization, mostly Zulu.

Kaffir: South African derogatory term for Africans, comparable to "nigger."

Kaunda, Dr. Kenneth: President of Zambia.*

Khoikhoi: African ethnic group often called Hottentots; inhabited Cape Province area in the seventeenth century.

KwaNdebele: South African homeland. Scheduled for "independence."

Laager: Term applied to South African withdrawal within themselves for defensive purposes; formerly, a circle of oxcarts for defense.

Lesotho: Former British protectorate of Basutoland. Independent 1966.

Luthuli, Chief Albert (c. 1898–1967): African nationalist leader; deposed from chiefdom by South African government; head of ANC for ten years. Won Nobel Peace Prize in 1960.

Machel, Samora: First President of Mozambique and Leader of FRELIMO, killed in plane crash, October 1986.

Malawi: Former British territory of Nyasaland. Independent 1964.

Mandela, Nelson: Leader of ANC, serving life sentence in South Africa.*

---

*Office held at time of publication.

Mandela, Winnie: ANC leader, banned for more than twenty years.

Moose, Richard: U.S. Assistant Secretary of State for African Affairs in the Carter administration.

Motlana, Dr. Ntatho: Leader of Soweto Committee of 10.*

Movement for the Liberation and Preservation of White South Africa: One of a number of white, pro-apartheid South African groups.

Mozambique: Former Portuguese territory. Independent 1975.

Mugabe, Robert: Prime Minister of Zimbabwe.* Leader of ZANU-PF.

Namibia: Generally accepted name for former German territory of South West Africa.

Natal: One of the four provinces of South Africa.

National Forum: Organization of Black Consciousness groups.

National Party: Party in power in South Africa. Founded by and controlled by Afrikaners but has other white members.

National Union for the Total Independence of Angola (UN-ITA): Guerrilla organization contesting for power in Angola.

Naudé, Beyers: Dutch Reformed minister. General Secretary of SACC.* Founded Christian Institute. Was banned for seven years.

New Conservative Party: Right-wing political party, merged into the Conservative Party of South Africa in 1982.

New Republic Party: Minor South African political party with eight seats in Parliament in 1981 election. "Center" group.

Nujoma, Sam: President of SWAPO.*

Nyerere, Julius: First President of Tanzania, retired. Active leader of frontline states.

---

*Office held at time of publication.

Nzo, Alfred: General Secretary of ANC.*

Orange Free State: One of the four provinces of South Africa.

Organization of African Unity (OAU): Continental association of independent African states, founded in 1963.

Ovambo: Largest ethnic group in Namibia.

Pan Africanist Congress (PAC): South African liberation organization, founded in 1959. Robert Sobukwe, who died in 1978, was the first President.

Parastatals: Corporations owned and controlled by the South African government.

Pass, passbook (reference book): Document formerly required to be carried by all adult Africans; included permission for presence in area.

Popular Movement for the Liberation of Angola (MPLA): Political party in power in Angola.

Population Registration Act: Law requiring classification of South Africans by race.

Program to Combat Racism: Section of WCC which made grants from special funds to southern African liberation movements for humanitarian purposes.

Progressive Federal Party: Political party in South Africa combining the former Progressive Party and the liberal elements of the United Party. The official opposition.

Prohibition of Political Interference Act: Now repealed, formerly prohibited interracial political party membership.

Quaker Peace and Service: International service agency of London and Ireland Yearly Meetings of Religious Society of Friends.

Rand: Unit of South African currency. Equal to $0.44 U.S., October 24, 1986.

---

*Office held at time of publication.

Reserves: Early name for bantustans or homelands, still has some usage.

Rhodes, Cecil (1853–1902): British pioneer who opened territory in central Africa for the British Empire. Founder of Rhodesia (now Zimbabwe).

Rhodesian Front: Party in power during the Unilateral Declaration of Independence in Southern Rhodesia (now Zimbabwe).

Robben Island: Maximum-security prison for political prisoners in bay near Cape Town.

San: African ethnic group often called Bushmen; inhabited Cape Province area in the seventeenth century.

Savimbi, Jonas: Leader of UNITA.*

Slabbert, Frederik van zyl: Former leader of the Progressive Federal Party.

Sobukwe, Robert: Founder of PAC. Died 1978.

Sotho: One of the three largest ethnic groups in South Africa.

South African Digest: Publication of the South African Department of Foreign Affairs and Information.

South African Institute of Race Relations: Voluntary organization with headquarters in Johannesburg. Good reputation for research of factual information. Works to improve race relations in South Africa.

South African Student Movement (SASM): Activist Black Consciousness organization of high school students.

South African Students' Organization (SASO): Organization of black university students.

Southern African Development Coordination Conference (SADDC): Organization of southern African independent states

---

*Office held at time of publication.

except South Africa, plus Tanzania, to promote development and economic cooperation.

South West Africa: Namibia.

Soweto (South West Townships): African township outside of Johannesburg.

Soweto Committee of 10: Leadership group which grew out of 1976 Soweto uprising.

Sullivan, Leon: Baptist minister in Philadelphia, member of the Board of Directors of General Motors, initiator of Sullivan code of conduct.*

Survey of Race Relations: Annual report of data by SAIRR.

Suzman, Helen: Longtime member of South African Parliament and opponent of apartheid.

Swaziland: Former British protectorate. Independent 1968.

Tambo, Oliver: President of ANC,* in exile.

Tanzania: East African country, active on southern African issues. Formed from union of former territories of Tanganyika and Zanzibar in 1964.

Transkei: South African homeland. "Independent" 1976.

Transvaal: One of the four provinces of South Africa.

Tutu, Bishop Desmond: Archbishop of Cape Town and Metropolitan of the Church of the Province of Southern Africa.* Won Nobel Peace Prize in 1984.

Unilateral Declaration of Independence (UDI): Southern Rhodesian declaration of independence by Ian Smith, then Prime Minister, 1965.

United National Independence Party (UNIP): Ruling party in Zambia.

Union of South Africa: Former name (1910–61) of the Republic of South Africa.

---

*Office held at time of publication.

Venda: South African homeland. "Independent" 1979.

Xhosa: One of the three largest African ethnic groups in South Africa.

Zambia: Former British territory of Northern Rhodesia. Independent 1964.

Zimbabwe African National Union (Patriotic Front) (ZANU-PF): Ruling party in Zimbabwe.

Zulu: One of the three largest African ethnic groups in South Africa.

Selected References

Abrahams, Peter. *A Night of Their Own.* New York: Alfred A. Knopf, 1965.

Africa News (Durham, N.C.). Biweekly issues.

Albright, David, ed. *Communism in Africa.* Bloomington: Indiana University Press, 1980.

American Friends Service Committee. *Namibia.* Philadelphia, 1982.

———. *South Africa: Challenge and Hope.* 1st ed. Philadelphia, 1982.

Amnesty International USA. *South Africa: Imprisonment under the Pass Laws.* New York, 1986.

André, Brink. *A Dry White Season.* New York: William Morrow, 1980.

Bernstein, Hilda. *For Their Triumphs and Their Tears.* London: International Defense and Aid Fund, 1975, 1978, 1985.

Biko, Steve. *I Write What I Like.* San Francisco: Harper & Row, 1978.

Boesak, Allan. *Walking on Thorns.* Grand Rapids, Mich.: Eerdmans, 1984.

British Council of Churches. *Political Change in South Africa: Britain's Responsibility.* London, 1979.

———. *Whose Rubicon?* London, 1986.

Brutus, Dennis. *A Simple Lust.* New York: Hill and Wang, 1973.

———. *Stubborn Hope.* Washington, D.C.: Three Continents Press, 1978.

Carter, Gwendolen. *Which Way Is South Africa Going?* Bloomington: Indiana University Press, 1980.

Catholic Institute for International Relations. *South Africa in the 1980s: State of Emergency.* 3rd ed. London, 1986.

Cock, Jacklyn. *Maids and Madams: A Study in the Politics of Exploitation.* Johannesburg: Ravan Press, 1980.

Coetze, J. M. *Waiting for the Barbarians.* New York: Penguin Books, 1980.

Frankel, Philip H. *Pretoria's Praetorians: Civil-Military Relations in South Africa.* New York: Cambridge University Press, 1984.

Fredrickson, George M. *White Supremacy: A Comparative Study in American and South African History.* New York: Oxford University Press, 1981.

Frederikse, Julie. *South Africa: A Different Kind of War.* London: Currey; Johannesburg: Ravan, 1986.

Fugard, Athol, John Kani, and Winston Ntshona. *Siswe Bansi Is Dead* and *The Island.* New York: Viking, 1973.

Gandhi, M. K. *Satyagraha in South Africa.* Stanford, Calif.: Academic Reprints, 1954.

Gerhart, Gail M. *Black Power in South Africa: The Evaluation of an Ideology.* Berkeley: University of California Press, 1979.

Hanlon, Joseph. *Mozambique: Revolution under Fire.* London: Zed Books, 1984.

Haysom, Nicholas. *Apartheid's Private Army: The Rise of the Right-Wing Vigilantes in South Africa.* London: Catholic Institute of International Relations, 1986.

Hirson, Baruch. *Year of Fire, Year of Ash.* London: Zed Books, 1979.

Hope, Marjorie, and James Young. *South African Churches in a Revolutionary Situation.* Maryknoll, N.Y.: Orbis Books, 1981.

International Defense and Aid Fund. *Women under Apartheid.* London, 1981.

Investors Responsibility Research Center. *Foreign Investment in South Africa.* Washington, D.C., current updates.

Joubert, Elsa. *The Long Journey of Poppie Nongena.* Johannesburg: Jonathon Bell, 1980.

Kairos Theologians. *Challenge to the Church: A Theological Comment on the Political Crisis in South Africa.* Braamfontein, 1985.

Kaunda, Kenneth. *The Riddle of Violence.* San Francisco: Harper & Row, 1980.

Labor Research Association. *Labor and South Africa.* July–August 1985 issue of *Economic Notes* (New York).

Lelyveld, Joseph. *Move Your Shadow: South Africa Black and White.* New York: Times Books, 1985.

Lewin, Hugh. *Bandiet.* London: Heinemann, 1974.

Lewin, Julius. *Politics and Law in South Africa: Essays on Race Relations.* London: Merlin, 1963.

Luthuli, Albert. *Let My People Go: The Autobiography of a Great African Leader*. Johannesburg: Collins, 1962.

Mandela, Nelson. *No Easy Walk to Freedom*. New York, Basic Books, 1965.

Mandela, Winnie. *Part of My Soul Went with Him*. New York: Norton, 1985.

Mathabane, Mark. *Kaffir Boy*. New York: Macmillan, 1986.

Minogue, Martin, and Judith Molloy, eds. *African Aims and Attitudes: Selected Documents*. London: Cambridge University Press, 1974.

Mzimele, Sipo E. *Apartheid: South African Naziism*. New York, Vantage, 1983.

NARMIC/AFSC. *Automating Apartheid*. Philadelphia, 1982.

———. *Investing in Apartheid: A Guide to U.S. Corporations in South Africa*. Philadelphia, 1985.

Nash, Margaret. *Black Uprooting from "White" South Africa: The Fourth and Final Stage of Apartheid*. Braamfontein: SACC, 1980.

Neuhaus, Richard John. *Dispensations in the Future of South Africa as South Africans See It*. Grand Rapids, Mich.: Eerdmans, 1986.

O'Brien, Conor Cruise. "What Can Become of South Africa?" *The Atlantic Monthly*, March 1986.

Paton, Alan. *Hope for South Africa*. New York: Praeger, 1959.

———. *Ah, But Your Land Is Beautiful*. New York: Scribner's, 1981.

Rotberg, Robert I. *Suffer the Future: Policy Choices in Southern Africa*. Cambridge: Harvard University Press, 1980.

Seidman, Ann. *The Roots of Crisis in South Africa*. Trenton: Africa World Press, 1985.

Seidman, Judy. *Ba Ye Zwa, The People Live; South Africa: Daily Life under Apartheid*. Boston: South End Press, 1978.

South African Institute of Race Relations. *Race Relations News* (Johannesburg). Monthly.

———, *Survey of Race Relations*. Annual.

South African Ministry of Information. *Backgrounder Reports* (Pretoria). Occasional issues.

———. *South African Digest* (Pretoria). Weekly.

Stockwell, John. *In Search of Enemies*. New York: Norton, 1978.

Study Commission on U.S. Policy Toward Southern Africa. *South Africa: Time Running Out*. New York: University of California Press, for the Foreign Policy Study Foundation, 1981.

Tutu, Desmond. *Hope and Suffering*. Grand Rapids, Mich.: Eerdmans, 1984.

Ungar, Sanford, and Peter Vale. "South Africa: Why Constructive Engagement Failed." *Foreign Affairs,* Winter 1985–86.

United Nations Economic Commission for Africa. *Women and Apartheid in South Africa and Namibia.* Addis Ababa, 1985.

Van der Merwe, H. W., et al. *African Perspectives on South Africa: A Collection of Speeches, Articles and Documents.* Cape Town: David Phillip, 1978.

Volman, Daniel. *A Continent Besieged: Foreign Military Activities in Africa.* Washington, D.C.: Institute of Policy Studies Report, 1980.

Wilson, Monica, and Leonard Thompson. *The Oxford History of South Africa.* New York and Oxford: Oxford University Press. Vol. I, 1969; Vol. 2, 1971.

Wiseman, Henry, and Alastair M. Taylor. *From Rhodesia to Zimbabwe: The Politics of Transition.* New York: Pergamon Press, 1978.

Woods, Donald. *Biko.* London: Paddington Press, 1978.

———. *Asking for Trouble.* New York: Atheneum, 1981.

Wilkins, Ivor, and Hans Strydom. *Broederbond: The Super-Afrikaners.* London: Transworld Publishers, 1979.

Ya-Otto, John. *Battlefront Namibia.* Westport, Conn.: Lawrence Hill, 1981.

Miscellany

The items that follow will be of particular interest to some readers of *South Africa: Challenge and Hope.*

RACE CLASSIFICATION

Two of Petra's teachers had asked to be present and volunteered their assurances that Petra Albertyn was one of the finest—Dr. Sterk cut them off: "We're not testifying to her quality. We're interested only in her race." And the way in which he spoke these words conveyed the clear impression that he now considered the accusations against this child justified. This encouraged the vice-principal to say that he had been watching Petra for some time, and she not only looked suspiciously dark, but she also behaved in distinctly Coloured ways.

"What do you mean?" Dr. Sterk asked.

"The way she says certain words."

Venloo's dominee, Reverend Classens, was a committee member and he asked ponderously, "Do we appreciate what we're doing here tonight? This child's entire future is at stake." "No one could be more sympathetic than we are, Dominee," Dr. Sterk said. "But if she is Coloured, then one of her parents must be Coloured, too. They can have a future among their own people. Not here in Venloo."

"Does this mean," the dominee asked, "that you plan to examine every child who seems a bit dark?"

"They are examined every day. By their fellow students. By everyone who sees them. This is a Christian nation, Dominee, and we obey the law."

"That is what I preach. But I also preach, 'Suffer the little children to . . . ' "

"We don't persecute little children. But we must keep serious priorities in mind."

"Such as?"

"The moral welfare of every child in this school."

After the meeting a grim-faced Dr. Sterk went to see the van Valcks, and reported: "I've seen the Albertyns and there is foundation for your accusations. The vice-principal has also had suspicions."

"That's what we told you," Mrs. van Valck said smugly. "What are you going to do about it?"

"I've asked the Albertyns to remove their daughter."

"And they refused?"

"They have." There was a long pause, in which each of the three considered the inevitable next step, the one that would throw the Community into turmoil. Twice Dr. Sterk made as if to speak, then thought better of it. In a matter of such gravity the decision must be made by people involved, and he would wait upon them.

Finally Leopold van Valck asked in a low voice, "You want to know whether we're prepared to lodge formal charges?"

"We are," his wife interrupted with great force. Having made the decision for all of them, she sat primly in her chair, hands folded, chin jutting out as if she were already bringing her testimony before the Race Classification Board.

—James A. Michener, *The Covenant* (New York: Random House, 1980), p. 748.

AN INTERVIEW

Dr. Slabbert: I can see from the Government's position that there are people with whom it cannot immediately talk in public. I am talking of, say, Buthelezi and even ANC members.

State President: But nothing prevents Buthelezi from talking to me.

Dr. Slabbert: Well, he's in a tremendous vice . . .

State President: I will tell you what Buthelezi's problem is. Buthelezi's problem is that he wants to talk alone, but does not want to talk together with other Black people.

Dr. Slabbert: Yes, there is a problem there, there is a problem, but that problem can be surmounted.

State President: How?

Dr. Slabbert: He must, as the English say, "be locked into an initiative." And I have a very strong feeling that we are on the threshold of such an initiative into which he can be drawn.

But you see, if you tell me of the development and the economy I can't fault it and I can only support it.

State President: I told Buthelezi, what the Zulu people need in the first place are not just political rights, because you have that. You can talk to me whenever you wish. But what you need in the first place is that the Tugela areas, that we develop the low-lying areas of the Tugela . . . He agreed with me.

Dr. Slabbert: Yes, I'm sure he agreed with you.

State President: But why does he not come and talk about that?

Dr. Slabbert: His problem lies on a symbolic level. His problem lies on the whole symbolic level. You see, Buthelezi and the ANC are busy eating each other. I mean they are going for each other, it is just unbelievable how they are going for each other.

State President: Yes, that is all they are doing.

Dr. Slabbert: They are stomping each other and Buthelezi says . . . and I told you at the beginning of the year his big problem is that if Mandela dies in jail he becomes the Muzorewa of South Africa and he is aware of that. He is scared of that. But it is not just that which he is scared of. At the moment the ANC is busy with a terribly strong anti-Buthelezi campaign, and why? Precisely for the reasons you have mentioned. The ANC wants to be the only bull in the kraal. And Buthelezi wants to be the only bull in the kraal.

State President: And they can't.

Dr. Slabbert: They can't. I mean I told both of them that there are many more bulls in the kraal than they were aware of . . .

—Transcript of a conversation between State President P. W. Botha and Frederik van zyl Slabbert (former leader of the Progressive Federal Party, the official opposition), November 25, 1985; printed in a supplement to the *South African Digest,* February 28, 1986.

EXCERPTS FROM THE KAIROS DOCUMENT

The KAIROS document is a Christian, biblical and theological comment on the political crisis in South Africa today. It is an attempt by concerned Christians in South Africa to reflect on the situation of death in our country. It is a critique of the current theological models that determine the type of activities the Church engages in to try to resolve the problems of the country. It is an attempt to develop, out of this perplexing situation, an alternative biblical and theological model that will in turn lead to forms of activity that will make a real difference to the future of our country.

* * *

The time has come. The moment of truth has arrived. South Africa has been plunged into a crisis that is shaking the foundations and there is every indication that the crisis has only just begun and that it will deepen and become even more threatening in the months to come. It is the KAIROS or moment of truth not only for apartheid but also for the Church.

* * *

The oppressive South African regime will always be particularly abhorrent to Christians precisely because it makes use of Christianity to justify its evil ways. As Christians we simply cannot tolerate this blasphemous use of God's name and God's Word.

* * *

There we sit in the same Church while outside Christian policemen and soldiers are beating up and killing Christian children or torturing Christian prisoners to death while yet other Christians stand by and weakly plead for peace. The Church is divided and its day of judgment has come.

* * *

The State makes use of the concept of law and order to maintain the status quo which it depicts as "normal." But this law is the unjust and discriminatory laws of apartheid and this order is the organised and institutionalised disorder of oppression.

* * *

We all know how the South African State makes use of the label "communist." Anything that threatens the status quo is labelled "communist." Anyone who opposes the State and especially anyone who rejects its theology is simply dismissed as a "communist." No account is taken of what communism really means. No thought is given to why some people have indeed opted for communism or for some form of socialism. Even people who have not rejected capitalism are called "communists" when they reject "State Theology." The State uses the label "communist" in an uncritical and unexamined way as its symbol of evil.

* * *

At the very heart of the gospel of Jesus Christ and at the very centre of all true prophecy is a message of hope. Nothing could be more relevant and more necessary at this moment of crisis of South Africa than the Christian message of hope.

* * *

There is hope. There is hope for all of us. But the road to that hope is going to be very hard and very painful. The conflict and the struggle will have to intensify in the months and years ahead because there is no other way to remove the injustice and oppression. But God is with us. We can only learn to become the instruments of his peace even unto death. We must participate in the cross of Christ if we are to have the hope of participating in his resurrection.

QUAKERS IN SOUTH AFRICA

The Society of Friends has been active in the nineteenth and twentieth centuries in South Africa, although always with few members. Early-nineteenth-century British settlers in the Cape Province included some Quakers. Much later English Quakers developed commercial, business, and humanitarian interests in the Transvaal and Natal provinces. Some Quakers came as educators.

One notable Friend was Richard Gush, who, like William Penn in Pennsylvania, maintained cordial and fair relations with the indigenous inhabitants from the time of his arrival in 1820. His memory and record are appreciated by many, including non-Quakers. The respect he won gave him the opportunity on occasion to halt or prevent hostilities between whites and blacks. He was recognized as a friend of the blacks, and he provided them with food in times of hunger.

A small British delegation of Quakers who visited in southern Africa before 1840 recognized the need for blacks and whites to have better facilities for living and working together. They raised special funds for the Lovedale Mission in the eastern Cape. It needed a better water system, so their funds created a "furrow" to conduct a stream from the Chiume (Tyiume) River to the Station. This has recently been replaced by a modernized system. The delegation established a Quaker Meeting for worship in Cape Town in 1838, which functioned at least for the two years they were present, according to the journal of James Backhouse. Backhouse also founded a school for white and coloured children, which was funded by English Friends and operated from 1840 to 1879. The present Meeting in Cape Town was started in 1903 and was approved by the London Yearly Meeting in 1906.

British Quakers' opposition to the Anglo-Boer War and their profound sympathy for the suffering of the Boer civilians is remembered in some of the Afrikaner patriotic museums. In this, Friends worked closely with Emily Hobhouse and her Anglican colleagues. The collection and return of many family Bibles, looted from Boer farms during the war and taken to England by soldiers, is still recalled with gratitude. The Bibles held vital family records as well as being important guides for the Boers' Christian piety. English Friends established and administered a relief fund which South African members also supported.

The Johannesburg Meeting for Worship began in 1912 in the YMCA; it was recognized by London Friends in 1917. The present-day Southern Africa Yearly Meeting includes groups in several adjacent countries and was formally organized in 1946. The South Africa General Meeting includes congregations and small groups gathering in various parts of the country. The Meeting in Soweto has grown slowly since the early 1960s and now has a center under construction which will provide some services to the community.

Within South Africa today there are fewer than two hundred Quakers, mostly white and English-speaking. Their work is extensive in light of their few members.

The Quaker Service Fund, which operates nonracially, is notably active in Johannesburg and the Cape, with especially elaborate and personalized activities on behalf of the country's black population, who suffer political and economic injustice and for whom little exists in the way of general social services. The continued Quaker opposition to the evils and hardships of the apartheid system and to the militarization of the countryside is notable. Quakers, like many other Christian groups, tend to be fragmented and divided on some issues, but what they do is of considerable value. Friends are, however, the first to admit how limited their concerns and efforts can be, compared to the need.

AFSC POLICY ON SOUTH AFRICA

On September 28, 1985, the Board of Directors of the American Friends Service Committee approved a statement of policy on South Africa that includes the following points:

1. One person, one vote, in a unitary nation of South Africa is the principle against which all political changes in South Africa must be measured. This principle precludes definition of groups by race for political representation, and requires that the homelands policy be abandoned.

2. In this context, it is clear that apartheid must be abolished. It is not a system that can be reformed. Changes that represent gradual repeal or modification of apartheid's excesses while leaving in place its fundamental structures will have little effect on the lives of the majority of South Africans. Meaningful change requires comprehensive repeal of all of apartheid's legal underpinnings. . . .

3. The United States must establish supportive relationships with all South Africans who are seeking to build a new, nonracial nation. Pursuit of change solely through engagement with the minority government, whether that engagement is "constructive" or critical, serves to undergird that government and help postpone the inevitable and necessary shifts in political power. The result will be prolonged suffering and bloodshed.

4. South Africa's illegal occupation of the U.N. Trust Territory of Namibia and military incursions and destabilization of the economic, political and social structures of neighboring countries are required to defend its domestic apartheid policies. The United States must exert leadership in seeking the end to such South African intervention.

5. Beyond apartheid's abolition, the goal of justice, stability and peace in southern and South Africa requires a profound redress of the vast disparities of wealth and power that have been the legacy of apartheid and centuries of exploitation. The United States must

use its influence to support fundamental economic and political transitions. . . .

6. The United States has long intervened in South Africa in pursuit of its own economic and geopolitical objectives and in ways that have benefited South Africa's privileged white minority. It must now redirect its heavy influence in the interest of justice and peace. Economic sanctions that are strictly implemented are one necessary component of such a redirected policy.

7. There is no valid basis for continued support of the South African government on grounds of anti-communism. The issue is not communism; it is injustice. The excesses under the current emergency decree have made ever plainer the violence and injustice that have always been integral to the apartheid system. The sooner that system is abolished, the greater the chance that what follows will be a just, non-racial, participatory system of government.

8. Economic ties between the United States and South Africa continue to provide vital support to the apartheid system and, at the same time, provide individuals and institutions in this country with financial benefits from that system. Both the support and the benefits must be ended. Divestment by individuals, by private groups and by government bodies is an important step in this direction.